THE
HULL CITY
MISCELLANY

THE
HULL CITY
MISCELLANY

DAVID CLAYTON

First published 2009
This new edition in paperback first published in 2012

The History Press
The Mill, Brimscombe Port
Stroud, Gloucestershire, GL5 2QG
www.thehistorypress.co.uk

British Library Cataloguing in Publication Data.
A catalogue record for this book is available from the British
Library.

ISBN 978 0 7524 8627 7

Typesetting and origination by The History Press
Printed in Great Britain
Manufacturing managed by Jellyfish Print Solutions Ltd

*For Ryan Sheppard and in memory of his grandfather,
John Leonard – young and old Tigers together*

ACKNOWLEDGEMENTS

It has been a real joy to write this book and a privilege to find out more about the club and thanks must go to a number of superfans, some incredible statisticians and one of the most detailed websites I've ever come across. I hope the majority of Hull folk will enjoy this.

Briefly, thanks to Andy Beill who, probably unknowingly, was sent to Earth to help make my life so much easier by creating an incredibly detailed document containing everything there is to know about the Tigers, statistically speaking. Thanks also to Michelle Tilling, my editor at The History Press, Will Unwin, Alex Rowen, Chris Sheppard and special thanks, as always, to my wife Sarah and our three beautiful young children, Harry, Jaime and Chrissie. That's pretty much it – for facts and figures from elsewhere, thanks as well. You know who you are.

David Clayton, August 2012

FOREWORD

by Brian Horton

I first joined Hull City as player/manager in 1984 and up to 2010, I was still involved with the club as Phil Brown's number two – something I consider to have been a great privilege. I've enjoyed reading *The Hull City Miscellany* and I must admit it's been a bit of an eye-opener and it shows how steeped in history this club really is.

The people of Hull have always been good to me so to be part of a team that helped bring Premier League football to Humberside is hugely satisfying. The fans were great with me first time around but the past two seasons, playing in front of packed houses at the KC Stadium, have surpassed my first spell and the supporters are enjoying it just as much as we are.

Obviously there are still numerous events and facts that won't have found their way into this book – there's only so much room after all – so I'll share a memory that is probably unique to me. We'd just won promotion at Walsall, which was doubly satisfying for me, because they'd given me a free transfer as a kid. Chairman Don Robinson was ecstatic and he came on to the pitch to celebrate with our fans, before coming over to me and saying, 'Jump on my back and I'll run you round to our fans, Brian!'

I politely turned him down, though I could imagine what it would have looked like if I'd have let him – what a character. I think Don once hired a camel or an elephant to walk around the pitch at Boothferry Park, too – he was always full of ideas and enthusiasm for the club and that kind of attitude is infectious, believe me.

I hope you enjoy this book as it lends a fascinating insight into what makes Hull City tick and for me, that's our supporters.

Brian Horton

FIXED PENALTY NOTICE

When it comes to penalty shoot-outs, generally speaking, City are pants. In fact, no self-respecting supporter of the Tigers would ever back their team to come out on top if a match went to the dreaded spot-kick drama to settle the game.

Of course, City entered the history books when they lost a Watney Cup tie to Manchester United in 1970. With the scores level after extra time, the match became the first on English soil to be settled by a shoot-out and the scene was set for 30 years of misery when United edged the game 4–3 at a packed Boothferry Park. It would be 17 years before City were again forced to settle a match this way, losing a League Cup tie against Charlton Athletic 5–4 on penalties at Selhurst Park.

Then, in November 1995, the Tigers again failed to roar from a penalty shoot-out, losing 3–1 to Wrexham in an FA Cup first-round replay. An Associate Members' Cup (Auto Windscreens Shield) tie against Rochdale became City's fourth failure in 2000 when, after a 0–0 draw in normal and added time couldn't separate the teams, Dale edged the spot-kicks 5–4 to inflict a fourth consecutive loss on penalties. In 2004, the Tigers outdid themselves losing two penalty shoot-outs in the space of a month, firstly 3–1 to Wrexham in the League Cup and then 4–1 to Hartlepool in the Associate Members' Cup (LDV Vans Trophy) to make it six defeats on the bounce. Finally, at the seventh attempt, City won a shoot-out, beating Hartlepool 3–2 in 2007 in a League Cup second round tie at the KC Stadium.

Does this mean the curse has finally lifted? We'll have to wait until the next time the Tigers are involved in a penalty shoot-out to find out. . . .

HOW SWEET IT IS …

The Needler family assumed control of the Tigers in the late 1940s and were associated with City up until 1997 when former tennis player David Lloyd bought the club. The Needlers famously first introduced boiled sweets to Hull – and to the world – and for a time, the tooth-breaking candy was thrown out to the crowd prior to home matches.

RAIDERS OF THE FER ARK

Towards the end of Boothferry Park's days as the Tigers' home, the stadium became affectionately known by City fans as 'Fer Ark'. Owing to the lack of finances for repairs, the scoreboard didn't actually show the score throughout the matches towards the end of the club's tenure at the ground and the only letters that were illuminated on the large Boothferry Park sign were 'BoothFERry pARK.'

CAPITAL RESULT!

The Housemartins' 1986 album, *London 0 Hull 4*, arguably put the city of Hull on the nation's radar and during the 2008/09 Premier League season, the Housemartins' album took on a mystical aura when the Tigers recreated the record's title by beating Fulham, Tottenham, Arsenal and West Ham to make it four wins out of four against clubs from the capital. Art imitating life? Who knows, but the fact is, it really was London 0 Hull 4!

RECORD BREAKERS

Following the Tigers' successive promotions from the Fourth Division to the Second, local musicians Amber & Black celebrated by recording a song for the club – little did they know they'd have to wait 25 years to do a follow-up! On reaching the Premier League, Amber & Black released 'The City's On Fire' – here are the lyrics:

Time runnin' out, that was for definite
A sleeping giant with barely a breath in it
So-called saviours making a mess of it
They padlocked the gates . . . Thanks a lot!

A hundred years of not much to shout about
Not many days to truly be proud about
But now here's something to really get loud about
This party, it ain't gonna stop.

Oh, The City's on Fire
With a burnin' desire
Tiger's are roaring,
And destiny's calling
Cos now is the time
Yeah the City's on fire
We're goin' higher and higher
There's no turning back 'cos you're Amber and Black
Till you die, i-i-ie, i-i-ie.

Here we are, have we got a team again!
The KC Army daring to dream again
A tiger nation that's raring to scream again
And we're going to sing 'til we drop

(Repeat chorus)

H-U-L-L C-I-T-Y
H-U-L-L C-I-T-Y
H-U-L-L C-I-T-Y
H-U-L-L
C-I-T-Y
H-U-L-L C-I-T-Y
H-U-L-L C-I-T-Y
H-U-L-L C-I-T-Y
H-U-L-L
C-I-T-Y
. . . That's all we need

(Repeat chorus)

The sleeping giant with barely a breath in it
Time runnin' out, that was for definite
But heroes came, making the best of it
The tigers are back. Fancy that!

© Amber & Black

TIGER BEAT

There are several songs City have run out to prior to home matches over the years. Mud's 'Tiger Feet' was the choice in the 1970s, while Survivor's 1980s No.1 'Eye of the Tiger' inspired one or two Rocky-esque displays by the hosts. 'Tiger, Tiger Burning Bright' is another offering, though Phil Brown's version of the Beach Boys' classic 'Sloop John B' will take some beating!

GRIM UP NORTH!

Celebrity Tigers fans are few and far between, but anyone who grew up in the 1970s will be relieved to hear that Basil Brush's human sidekick, Roy North, is a City fan.

YOU CAN CALL ME, AL

During the 1994/95 Third Division campaign, City were going through something of an injury crisis. Boss Terry Dolan was so desperate for outfield players that he named second-choice goalkeeper Alan Fettis as one of his outfield subs for the home game against Oxford United on 17 December 1994.

With City leading 2–1, Fettis made his entrance from the bench and within minutes had extended the Tigers' lead and secured all three points!

However, the story doesn't end there; the popular Fettis, who played more than 100 times during a five-year stint with City, repeated the feat. In the final match of the same campaign, Dolan handed Fettis the no. 8 shirt for an away trip to Blackpool. With the match poised at 1–1 and the game entering its final minute, up popped Fettis to net the winner – no wonder the fans loved the big Northern Irishman.

CROUCHING TIGERS, HIDDEN MEANING?

You'll probably already know this entry so let's get it done and dusted straight away – Hull City is the only team in the English Football League which hasn't got a single letter that you can colour in – but the real mystery is, which anorak took the time to discover this to be true?

REWRITING THE RECORD BOOKS ...

Up to 2008, the nation's favourite trivia quiz question was: which is the largest city in England to have never had a team in the top division? The answer, of course, was Hull – but promotion in May 2008 rendered the question defunct and the search is now on for an updated version of the said question.

GEO THE FIRST

Geovanni Deiberson Maurício Gómez – 'Geo' to the City fans – has a number of notable firsts and records under his belt for the Tigers. The first Brazilian to play for the club and, with in excess of £23m spent on the player during his career to date, he is also the most expensive talent the club has ever had, though cost manager Phil Brown nothing after he signed from Manchester City on a free transfer in 2008. Capped five times by Brazil, he was the first player to join Hull City as a Premier League club and he wrote his name into the history books by scoring the club's first Premier League goal when he struck home a 23rd-minute equaliser against Fulham in August 2008 – and that game also led to him receiving City's first Premier League Man of the Match award.

Geo has proved a hugely popular signing for the fans and his spectacular goals during the Tigers' first campaign in the top-flight have ensured his place in City's folklore. Continuing his 'firsts' for the club, the former Barcelona and Benfica forward became the first Tiger to win *Match of the Day*'s Goal of the Month with his spectacular effort away to Arsenal – a goal that also won him the City supporters' Goal of the Season. Geo kept his fine personal record of goals scored against Manchester United when he scored a penalty at Old Trafford during a 4–3 defeat – he'd scored the winner for Manchester City against United the previous season and also scored against the Reds for Benfica in 2005. Geo had his contract cancelled by mutual consent in 2010 and moved to San Jose Earthquakes in the MLS where he became the club's first 'designated player' – whatever that means!

ROARY THE TIGER

Without doubt the best mascot in British football is City's Roary the Tiger. Roary became the club's mascot at the start of the 1999/2000 season, and was christened 'Roary' through a competition run in the matchday programme. Roary hit the headlines in November 1999 when he was sent off during an FA Cup first-round match at Hayes for causing trouble on the touchline. While the ref wasn't pleased with his behaviour, the City fans thought Roary was grrrreat. . . .

BROWNY SAID IT . . .

'We've survived and I can say it's the greatest achievement of my career.'

Forget the poor run, it was job done as far as the boss was concerened

'There would be no better man to replace Eriksson. Sam [Allardyce] would have no problems dropping big-name players.'

Browny comments on his old mate being in the running for the Man City job

'There was only one manager who wanted to win the game and that was me. Micky Adams came here for a draw and he got the result he wanted.'

Browny – not overly impressed by then Coventry boss Mickey Adams

'I was beginning to think either my managerial career or Pride Park was cursed.'

It was Pride Park, Phil. . . .

'A European place is the ultimate aim, either through winning a trophy or by way of position in the Premier League. I have got my personal ambitions, and all I can say is that I want to realise them in the near future.'

**Ambitious to the last – Tigers in Europe, Browny?
Why not?**

'The tension was unbearable. The score was only 1–0, both here and at Villa Park, and I was thinking, "Do we need to score a goal or can we afford to lose?" At half-time Steve Parkin said, "We need to score a goal here" and I must admit I did a double-take. It was a negative vibe that was unusual for me, but it was enough for us today.'

The Tigers boss relives that agonising but ultimately joyous final day of the 2008/09 Premier League campaign

'He was adamant he wanted to play, but I didn't think he was fit enough to play in the Premier League aged 40 – that was our difference of opinion.'

The Gaffer's verdict on Dean Windass' decision to join Oldham on loan and not Doncaster Rovers

CHEAP, WARM POP

Long before Peter Kay recalled the cheap pop his mum used to buy from the supermarket – namely 'Rolla Cola' – City chairman Don Robinson introduced the equally nasty-tasting Tiger Cola. Sold in a no-frills white plastic carton, Tiger Cola didn't go down well with City fans when it became available as the soft drink option at Boothferry Park and it disappeared before too long. Rumours that the chairman had been seen emptying Rolla Cola into plastic cartons prior to matches were never confirmed, though there was one thing the home support were sure of: Tiger Cola certainly didn't earn its stripes!

THE TIGERS HAVE NEVER WORN SPOTS ...

As the club's nickname depicts, Hull City have, for the majority of their existence, worn a 'Tigerish' kit using the colours black and amber. However, this has not always been the case and there have been many different versions over the years. The kits have gone from plain to garish, resulting in some of them being placed on unofficial 'Worst Kits in the History of Football' top tens.

For the first game that the club played, back in 1904, a plain white shirt was fashioned for the players. However, by the first full season the following year, a kit change had been agreed and a uniform consisting of black and amber shirts and black shorts was produced for the players.

This style continued up until the Second World War, apart from the 1935/36 season when the board decided to adopt the sky blue colours of the City of Hull. The move was met by protestations from the supporters and the amber and black was reinstated for the following season. The blue did return for a season after the Second World War, but again for only one campaign.

From the late 1940s onwards, stripes took a backseat as a plain shirt was developed and the side wore amber upon their torsos. The tiger element returned to the club's kit in the 1960s when stripes were reintroduced for four seasons, until the original idea of just having two horizontal black stripes placed across a gold shirt was put into practice. Like most extreme changes to the kits, this also only managed one season, and a stripe-less shirt was back for the following campaign.

Stripes went in and out of fashion throughout the 1970s and early '80s and the next major change to the tops was the addition of some red shoulder sections which lasted for five years from 1986 onwards.

The following decade brought some of football's most infamous outfits. In 1992, the club wore a kit which aimed to make the players look like a human version of City's nickname. A tigerskin shirt design was put in place and three seasons of hideous-looking kits ensued, as well as rumours that big game hunters were seen stalking the areas close to Boothferry Park. The kit was a disaster that only succeeded in bringing mild humour to opposition fans. Sanity prevailed and black and amber strips were once again employed from the mid-1990s onwards.

In recent times, a small amount of white has been incorporated into the shirts, but it has not been a staple of the kits since 2001. In 2004, for the club's centenary, it was decided that the shirt would resemble the one that was worn in their first season in the football league, and so a traditional black and amber striped kit was commissioned. Up to the 2011/12 season the side ran out in the 'norm' of black and amber stripes, but thankfully tigerskin seems to be out of fashion – for now at least. . . .

PLAY-OFFS

The fact that City made the Division Three 2000/01 play-offs at all was remarkable considering the Tigers were bottom of the league after nine games and on the brink of financial ruin. Brian Little somehow turned the club around and the push for the play-offs began, ironically, with a 1–0 win over Leyton Orient in February. With only two defeats since that result, City were the dark horses for promotion and faced Leyton

Orient in the play-off semi-finals. After John Eyre's 68th-minute goal settled the first leg, Orient fans must have wondered if their play-off curse had returned – two years earlier they had failed to score in both legs of their semi-final yet went through on penalties and in the final they again fired blanks, losing to Scunthorpe United. The second leg at Brisbane Road, however, saw Orient score goals in the 44th and 70th minutes to progress to the final and leave City fans with a tearful journey back to Humberside.

The Tigers' second experience of the play-offs was much more enjoyable. After an agonising last day in the Championship which saw City finish third and narrowly miss out on automatic promotion to Stoke, the Tigers faced Watford over two legs for a place at Wembley. With the first leg at Vicarage Road, Phil Brown's side knew they'd have to return home with something to aim for in the second leg, but few could have hoped for the 2–0 victory they actually got. After the hosts had a 4th-minute goal controversially rubbed off by the referee, veterans Nicky Barmby and Dean Windass both scored inside 23 minutes to leave City fans dreaming of an historic first Wembley appearance.

A packed KC Stadium was at fever pitch for the return match but it was Watford who scored first, on 12 minutes. However, goals from Barmby, Folan, Garcia and Doyle – the last three coming in the final 20 minutes – set up a final with Bristol City.

In front of 86,703 fans – the highest crowd the Tigers have ever played in front of – it was fitting that Dean Windass should score the only goal of the game, sending City into the Premier League for the first time.

10 THINGS YOU MIGHT NOT HAVE KNOWN ABOUT DEAN WINDASS

He may have moved on to pastures new, but Dean Windass will forever have a place in the hearts of every Hull City fan, with his winning play-off goal in 2008 guaranteeing him a place in club folklore. After dyeing his hair peroxide blond for the match, Deano put the Tigers into the Premier League for the first time in the club's 104-year history, with a 20-yard volley proving to be enough to beat Bristol City at Wembley – here are 10 facts about the big former Tigers No. 9.

- Deano was released by the Tigers as a youngster and was forced to pack peas for Bird's Eye and work on building sites as he dreamed of becoming a professional footballer – though he never lost sight of his goal.

- While playing for Bradford City, Deano received death threats following an awful two-footed jump-challenge on Bournemouth's Neil Young.

- Deano eventually joined the Tigers from local side North Ferriby United. City boss Terry Dolan offered the non-league outfit a 10 per cent cut of any sell-on fee and was true to his word – North Ferriby built an indoor sports centre with the £65,000 they received following Windass' move to Aberdeen.

- While at North Ferriby, Windass scored 21 goals in 18 appearances.

- Deano's testimonial was a match between Aberdeen and Hull City at the KC Stadium in August 2009. Aberdeen won 1–0 and almost 9,000 fans turned up.

- In the 2003 play-off final between Sheffield United and Wolves, Blades' boss Neil Warnock left Windass out of his squad and a disconsolate Deano spent the game drinking lager in his local instead.

- He was famously sent off three times in one game while playing for Aberdeen against Dundee. First he was shown a second yellow card, then he abused the referee, then he took out his fury on a corner flag and was ultimately banned for six games. Deano averaged nine bookings and one sending off a season before the 2008/09 campaign.

- Windass was born on April Fool's Day 1969. He hopes to play on beyond the age of 40 before moving into coaching.

- He quit the Tigers following a loan spell with Oldham Athletic and became player-assistant manager for Darlington.

- After a warts-and-all autobiography, *Deano: From Gipsyville to the Premiership*, in which he revealed his misery at Aberdeen and his numerous bust-ups with managers and authority, Deano upset some of his family so much that they no longer speak.

BADGE OF HONOUR

The first official club badge depicted a tiger in honour of the club's nickname. This has been the case for the majority of the time since the crest was first introduced in 1947. Nevertheless, certain changes have been made to the badge over the years. Firstly, the tiger design has been manipulated in many ways and slight moderations have been made to how the tiger is shown. For the inaugural version, a whole tiger was incorporated into the design, but this was then downsized to just the head of the furry beast, which was used until 1975 and the drastic change of just using the club initials as a representation of Hull City. Five years down the line, and the tiger's head was again placed upon the shirts of the side, and was kept as the crest until 1998 when the current logo was designed. Sanity prevailed and everyone was happy with badge which includes the club's official name and the words 'The Tigers'.

THE GAFFERS – A BRIEF HISTORY

Ever wondered which manager won the most games during their tenure or who had the shortest stay? Welcome to the managerial special section of *The Hull City Miscellany*. . . .

James Ramster, August 1904–April 1905
James Ramster was the very first manager of the football club, though his tenure lasted just eight months, all told. His only official games in charge were FA Cup preliminary ties against Stockton in which City drew 3–3 and lost the replay 4–1 – both games were played at the Victoria Ground.

Ambrose Langley, April 1905–April 1913
P: 318   W: 143   D: 67   L: 108

An experienced full-back who spent over a decade at Yorkshire rivals Sheffield Wednesday for whom he played in over 300 games, Langley enjoyed a successful time at the Tigers. During his first three years the club continuously finished in the top four of the Second Division and after eight seasons at the helm, he decided to move on, later managing Huddersfield Town.

Harry Chapman, April 1913–September 1914
P: 45   W: 20   D: 10   L: 15

The less famous of the Chapman brothers (his brother Herbert won the league with both Huddersfield and Arsenal), Harry spent the majority of his playing career at Sheffield Wednesday. While with the Owls, he won the FA Cup, but he ended his playing career at Hull and took on the managerial role at the beginning of the 1913 season. Chapman only spent one season in charge, and died in 1916 at the age of 37.

Fred Stringer, September 1914–July 1916
P: 43   W: 22   D: 6   L: 15

Fred Stringer was something of a stop-gap appointment by the Tigers following the enforced retirement of Harry Chapman and his record stands up well considering the difficult circumstances in which he inherited his position.

David Menzies, July 1916–July 1921 and in 1936
P: 114   W: 36   D: 35   L: 43

The club's first manager from north of the border, Menzies' professional playing career never really took off after time at Raith Rovers and he eventually moved onto Bradford City to further his career. He played very little for the Bantams, but soon began training the first team at Bradford, though his efforts were curtailed by the outbreak of the First World War. In 1916 he became the Hull City manager and spent five seasons with the club.

He left in 1921 to return to Bradford City and subsequently moved on again in 1926 to manage Doncaster Rovers. Menzies made a less prosperous return to the club in 1936, though sadly the Tigers were relegated and, more tragically, Menzies died during his second spell on Humberside.

Harold Percy Lewis, July 1921–January 1923
P: 71   W: 27   D: 18   L: 26

A largely average reign from Percy Lewis with his team not performing too badly during his 18-month tenure. He survived a dodgy start with four defeats in his first half-dozen games in charge – including a 6–0 reverse – to steady the ship and guide City to win their next five games in succession.

Billy McCracken, January 1923–May 1931
P: 375   W: 134   D: 104   L: 137

Northern Irishman Billy McCracken played for Newcastle United for almost two decades during a prosperous playing career. His legacy spreads wider than just the Magpies and thanks to the years he spent perfecting the art of the offside trap, the FA were forced to change the rules to give opposing strikers a fairer chance. He arrived at City in 1923 as manager and his most notable achievement in Humberside was taking the side to an FA Cup semi-final in 1930. Upon leaving, he took up a similar role at Gateshead FC, and later moved to Millwall and then Aldershot.

Haydn Green, May 1931–March 1934
P: 123   W: 61   D: 24   L: 38

An experienced manager who had managed Lincoln City prior to his arrival, as boss of the Tigers Green won almost half of his matches at the helm and guided the team to Third Division (North) title during his second year in charge.

Jack Hill, March 1934–January 1936
P: 77   W: 24   D: 15   L: 38

Jack Hill played for a variety of teams spanning the length and breadth of England, starting off at Durham City before moving down to Plymouth Argyle. His other clubs included Burnley, Newcastle and Bradford, though Hill's only success as a player was while with the Tigers who won the Third Division North in 1933.

Alas, in his role as manager he was far less successful. In the second year of his reign he took the club to the brink of relegation and was subsequently sacked. In 1948 he returned to the club as a scout and stayed on until 1955.

David Menzies, January 1936–December 1936
See earlier David Menzies entry.

Ernest Blackburn, December 1936–December 1946
P: 117   W: 50   D: 31   L: 36

Lancastrian by both name and birth, Ernie Blackburn is one of City's longest-serving managers with a decade of service under his belt. The Second World War cut short his promising reign in which City, while never promoted, were also never out of the top seven.

Frank Buckley, May 1946–March 1948
P: 80   W: 33   D: 19   L: 28

Commonly referred to as 'The Major' after leaving the Army to embark on a career as a footballer, Mancunian Frank Buckley had a nomadic start to his new profession, frequently moving between clubs in the early 1900s, playing for six different clubs and making 100 appearances. In 1914 he gained his one and only England cap, in a game against Ireland.

His managerial career made for even more interesting reading – he moved from East Anglia to Blackpool, and then onto Wolves, followed by Notts County, where he became Britain's highest paid manager, prior to arriving on Humberside. He had a lasting effect on football by creating a scouting network throughout England and Wales, something that was almost non-existent before this. Sadly, he left little legacy at Hull and left after two years at the helm, going on to manage Leeds and Walsall.

Raich Carter, March 1948–September 1951
P: 157   W: 74   D: 41   L: 42

Horatio Stratton Carter, better known as 'Raich', was a high quality footballer in his own right, making 13 appearances for England pre-Second World War. Carter also won the Division One Championship and FA Cup, which he did both pre- and post-war, making him quite unique in England.

He is known as being one of the greatest footballers in Hull City's history and as manager of the Tigers, he won the Division Three North. For many he will be remembered for bringing Don Revie to the club. Later on in his career he managed Leeds United and, impressively, he was a successful cricketer playing at county level for both Durham and Derbyshire.

Bob Jackson, June 1952–March 1955
P: 123   W: 42   D: 26   L: 55

Jackson made his name in management by winning the Division One title on two occasions with Portsmouth in the late 1940s and early 1950s. Unfortunately, he was unable to repeat that level of success with City, and left after three years of largely average results.

Bob Brocklebank, March 1955–May 1961
P: 302   W: 113   D: 71   L: 118

Bob Brocklebank only ever played professionally for two clubs, making a name for himself as an inside-right forward for both Aston Villa and Burnley. His first role as a manager was at Chesterfield where he successfully stabilised the club in Division Two before leaving for the top-flight Midlands outfit Birmingham City. After five years at St Andrew's, he decided to leave for pastures new, and took on the less pressurised role of a scout at West Brom. He was tempted back into management in 1955 by the Tigers who endured more lows than highs during his spell in charge, being relegated twice and promoted once. Brocklebank left the club in 1961 and took on his last managerial job at Bradford City.

Cliff Britton, July 1961–June 1970
P: 406   W: 170   D: 101   L: 135

Britton was a quality midfielder who spent the majority of his career providing crosses for the Everton legend Dixie Dean – a period that that included an FA Cup victory in 1933. This earned him a great reputation and saw him win nine caps for England. The likeable Bristolian then moved into a career in management, after the Second World War, when he was handed the reins at Burnley. He soon guided the Lancashire club to the First Division and also to an FA Cup final in 1947.

Britton was then given the chance of returning to Everton. After six years at Goodison Park he eventually resigned amid much fan and boardroom pressure. After leaving Merseyside, he took a break from football before being tempted back by Preston North End in 1956, where he guided them to the runners-up spot in the 1957/58 season. Britton was unable to maintain that level of success and eventually left the club in 1961 after being relegated to Division Two. Upon leaving

PNE, he took up a similar position at Boothferry Park. Due to a lack of funding he was forced to blood a lot of youngsters in his sides. In 1964 he brought future Hull legend Ken Wagstaff to the club and his young side won the Division Three title in 1966, but failed to push on from this and Britton left the club in 1970 after failing to take the club any further.

Terry Neil, June 1970–September 1974
P: 174   W: 61   D: 55   L: 58

The Belfast-born Terry Neil played over 270 games for Arsenal and also gained 59 caps for his home nation, scoring two goals. In 1970, after losing his place in the Gunners' side, he moved to Boothferry Park aged only 28, becoming the League's youngest manager. In his first season on Humberside, Neil took the club to sixth in the Second Division, City's highest post-war finish. He also enjoyed a similar role within the Northern Ireland set-up, and became the lead cap-winner at the time. Neil moved back to North London in 1974 in order to coach Arsenal's great rivals Tottenham Hotspur, but an unsuccessful spell at White Hart Lane seemingly endeared him even more to the Arsenal board who recruited him as their youngest ever manager, when he re-joined the club as a 34-year-old. His time at Arsenal was a successful one, in the cup competitions at least, reaching three consecutive cup finals, and losing to Valencia in the 1980 European Cup Winners' Cup final. The side then faltered and by 1983 Neil was unemployed and decided to retire from the game.

John Kaye, September 1974–October 1977
P: 126   W: 40   D: 40   L: 46

Kaye became West Brom's record signing when he joined the Midlands outfit from Scunthorpe for a fee of £44,750 in May 1963. Much to the delight of the Baggies' faithful

– and to Kaye himself – during his decade at the club he became an FA and League Cup winner, the latter in 1966. Although popular with the City supporters, his time in charge could hardly be described as successful, and after three seasons of mid-table football, Kaye handed on the managerial baton.

Bobby Collins, October 1977–February 1978
P: 19   W: 4   D: 7   L: 8

The pocket-sized Scotsman had an illustrious career that took in spells with Celtic, Everton and Leeds. He enjoyed great personal and team success during his career, including winning the Footballer of the Year award in 1965. Collins' international career saw him make 31 appearances for Scotland and score 10 goals. Injury ended his top-flight career and he was forced to make his living at a lower level with Bury, Oldham and in the Irish League, until he decided to try his hand at management. He worked at Huddersfield before moving on to City, where he managed only five months before being relieved of his duties. His final management role was at Barnsley and he ended his football career with coaching roles at Leeds and, later, in Australia.

Ken Houghton, April 1978–December 1979
P: 72   W: 23   D: 22   L: 27

A man of humble origins, Ken Houghton failed to make the grade at Sheffield United and instead went to work down the mines while still harbouring ambitions to play professionally. His dreams were realised when his local side, Rotherham United, signed him on, and Houghton later joined Hull where he played in the successful side of the mid-1960s. He became a fans' favourite through his dynamic passing and powerful shots. Houghton eventually left for Scunthorpe, followed by brief stints by the seaside at Scarborough and Bridlington with whom

Houghton moved into coaching. City then offered him the opportunity to take over a failing side, which he did with vigour, but he didn't bring any real success to the club, and was sacked in December 1979.

Mike Smith, December 1979–March 1982
P: 99   W: 27   D: 29   L: 43

Smith enjoyed an intriguing managerial career where he spent the majority of time at the helm of various national sides, including two periods in charge of Wales and another more exotic spell as Egypt's boss, where he guided his side to an African Cup of Nations victory. His time as City manager was mainly notable for taking the club into the Fourth Division for the first time in its history – an unwanted record that resulted in him leaving the club.

Bobby Brown, March 1982–June 1982
P: 19   W: 10   D: 4   L: 5

The former Scotland manager was a fixture on the Hull coaching staff under Mike Smith, but was promoted to a caretaker role after his dismissal. He only managed the club for three months, though his overall record suggests he perhaps deserved longer.

Colin Appleton, June 1982–May 1984 and May–October 1989
P: 107   W: 48   D: 37   L: 22

A Yorkshireman by birth, Appleton played for the first 12 years of his career at Leicester City where he was involved in over 270 matches for the Foxes. After success with his hometown club, Scarborough, Appleton was given the task of plotting the Tigers' escape from the bottom tier of the Football League. He achieved this with aplomb by finishing as runners-up in the Fourth Division with a club record tally of 90 points. After failing to gain a second successive promotion the following season by the merest fraction, Appleton resigned. He then spent time as manager with both Swansea City and Exeter City though he returned to Humberside for a brief, and unsuccessful, spell at the beginning of the 1989 season.

Brian Horton, June 1984–April 1988
P: 195   W: 77   D: 58   L: 60

'Nobby' Horton, the current assistant manager of the Tigers, was in charge for four years during the mid-1980s. In his first season at the helm he combined playing and managing the side and he succeeded where Colin Appleton had failed and took City up to the Second Division.

The team carried on their momentum into the following season, finishing sixth in the second tier. Unfortunately, the side struggled for the next two seasons, though Horton remained popular in the dressing room and on the terraces.

His sacking in 1988 shocked players and fans alike, though this didn't perturb Horton, who went on to lead the likes of Oxford United, Manchester City, Macclesfield and Huddersfield Town, before making a return to Humberside as assistant to Phil Brown.

Eddie Gray, June 1988–May 1989
P: 51   W: 13   D: 14   L: 24

A member of the famous Leeds side of the 1960s and '70s, Gray was a supremely talented winger in his day. He was a one-club man, making 454 appearances for the Yorkshire outfit, a career in which he managed just 12 caps for his native Scotland. In his final year as a player he combined on- and off-the-pitch duties in a player-manager role after Leeds had been relegated to the Second Division. However, after three unsuccessful seasons in charge at Elland Road, Gray left the club after 20 years of service.

He joined Hull in 1988 and had a positive impact in the early months of his reign. Alas, after one victory in the final 18 matches, he lost his job. After a few years of managing lower league clubs he was offered a position in the Leeds United youth set-up. In 2003 he was given the task of keeping a financially stricken Leeds in the Premier League, but failed to do so.

Colin Appleton, May–October 1989
See earlier entry.

Stan Ternent, November 1989–January 1991
P: 62   W: 19   D: 15   L: 28
A powerful midfielder from the North-East, Ternent started off at Burnley, before leaving for Carlisle where he played out the rest of his career. His first job in management was a disappointing one, lasting just 29 games at Blackpool before being sacked and he spent the next nine years learning his trade as part of the Bradford coaching team. In 1989, the Tigers gave him the opportunity to return to management. Again, his time as the top man proved troublesome and he was sacked three months prior to the side being relegated to the Third Division. Since leaving the club he has enjoyed a variety of managerial roles, and has been part of the backroom staff at several clubs. He enjoyed successive promotions in the mid-1990s as Bury manager and, up until November 2008, he was employed with Huddersfield Town.

Terry Dolan, January 1991–July 1997
P: 322   W: 99   D: 96   L: 127
Terry Dolan played in all four divisions of the Football League in a career that lasted 12 years. He turned out for Huddersfield Town, Bradford City and Rochdale, going on to manage the latter two. Dolan arrived at Boothferry Park in strange circumstances.

The club allegedly made an illegal approach for the then-Rochdale coach, but eventually a compensation package was agreed and the Yorkshireman continued with City, despite a disappointing record in which he took the club down twice in his six years in charge. As a leader, he was an unpopular figure, due to the club's descent down the league. However, he suffered also from the club's financial situation at the time, eventually leaving the Tigers in 1997.

Dolan went to manage both York City and Guiseley. In retrospect, he did a decent job in difficult circumstances at Hull.

Mark Hateley, July 1997–November 1998
P: 76   W: 17   D: 14   L: 45

The former England striker played across Europe during his career, enjoying spells with AC Milan and Monaco. Hateley's first move into management came when he accepted the chance to become player-manager at Boothferry Park. It was a difficult task due to the club's continuing poor financial situation and he (and the supporters) endured a 17-month period in which he enjoyed little success. Hateley was asked to leave the club when they were at the foot of the Third Division (old Fourth Division) and at risk of going out of the Football League altogether.

Warren Joyce, November 1998–April 2000
P: 86   W: 33   D: 25   L: 28

Warren Joyce made his name as a tenacious midfielder with several Lancashire clubs, including Bolton, Preston, and Burnley. He first arrived at City on a loan deal in 1995, and eventually signed permanently for the club in 1996. After Hateley left the club, Joyce became caretaker manager and was in charge of the club's great escape from what had seemed certain relegation to the

Conference. This brought him cult status among City fans, and he was then offered the job on a permanent basis, but was relieved of his duties within a year when the club decided to go for a more experienced manager. Since leaving the club he has managed in Belgium and is now part of Manchester United's backroom staff.

Brian Little, April 2000–February 2002
P: 97   W: 41   D: 28   L: 28

Brian Little was a one-club man, having made 247 appearances for Aston Villa over a 10-year period. He went on to manage them in the Premier League, the most successful period of his managerial career. Little came to City just after the start of the new millennium and was buoyed by the club's new ownership and an uncharacteristic wave of optimism around the place. Under his stewardship, the Tigers reached the Third Division play-off semi-finals in 2001, sadly losing out to Leyton Orient. The following season the club were on track to go up automatically, prior to the surprise resignation of Little who felt his future lay elsewhere. In recent years, he has had stints in charge of both Tranmere Rovers and Wrexham.

Jan Molby, April 2002–October 2002
P: 17   W: 2   D: 8   L: 7

The former Denmark international won the League Championship on two occasions with Liverpool and picked up 33 caps for Denmark so his pedigree as a player was without question. Molby started off brightly as a manager, winning the Conference with Kidderminster Harriers in 2000 and, due to this success, he was given the chance to manage the Tigers in 2002. Unfortunately for all concerned, his period in charge of the club was nigh-on disastrous, with only two victories in his brief spell in charge.

Peter Taylor, October 2002–June 2006
P: 184   **W: 77**   **D: 50**   **L: 57**

A former England international who also managed the national side for one match, Peter Taylor's time with the Tigers was a great success. Taylor brought City up to the newly-named League One, where he took them into the runners-up spot and consequently achieved promotion to the Championship. After finishing in 18th place, Crystal Palace, one of his former clubs, offered him the opportunity of returning to his beloved Selhurst Park as manager. He was unable to continue his success in London, and lasted only 18 months in the job. Taylor is currently in charge at Wycombe Wanderers.

Phil Parkinson, June 2006–December 2006
P: 24   **W: 5**   **D: 6**   **L: 13**

Phil Parkinson was an industrious midfielder who played over 350 games for Reading prior to moving to Colchester United to take up his first offer of management. After two seasons of mid-table finishes, Parkinson led the Essex club to an unlikely promotion to the Championship and, only weeks after achieving this feat, he left to join City. Unfortunately for both parties, he was unable to work his magic on Humberside and left after just six months in the job after a poor run of form, including a 5–1 defeat to his former employers Colchester. In recent years he has worked at Charlton as both assistant, and now manager.

Phil Brown, December 2006–March 2010
P: 157   **W: 52**   **D: 40**   **L: 65**

As a steady right full-back from South Shields, Brown played across the divisions during his playing career, eventually finishing with Blackpool in 1996. He then took the role of Sam Allardyce's assistant at the seaside club. Brown's former side Bolton then gave him the chance to move up the football league ladder, as he took a similar position as Colin Todd's number two. Even though Todd left the club in 1999, Brown stayed on as Allardyce, his former boss at Blackpool, came in to take the helm.

After almost 10 years on the coaching staff, Brown decided to start his own managerial career, taking on the top job at Derby County. Disappointingly, his first managerial position resulted in him being sacked after only seven months as the gaffer.

Unperturbed by the relative failure, Brown was offered a second opportunity to prove his worth in 2006, when he was appointed Hull City manager and in his first season he led the club to safety. However, there was no indication of what was in store for the Tigers faithful under Brown when, in his first full season in charge, he took the club to the Championship play-off final, where they defeated Bristol City at Wembley, winning promotion to the top flight for the first time. After a flying start to their Premier League campaign, Hull's form dipped in the second half of the season, surviving on the last day, though Brown, quite rightly, deemed this to be an even greater success than the previous campaign. However, in March 2010 Brown was placed on gardening leave and eventually replaced as manager of the Tigers. His spell as boss of City will remain one of the most successful of the modern era.

Iain Dowie, March 2010–June 2010
P: 9   W: 1   D: 3   L: 5
Dowie, employed as temporary 'Football Management Consultant', was charged with keeping the club in the Premier League at the end of the 2009/10 season.

Nigel Pearson, June 2010–November 2011
P: 64   W: 23   D: 20   L: 21
The former Sheffield Wednesday defender took over as Hull manager when he departed Leicester. Despite

starting the 2011/12 season well and only being a point off the play-offs at one stage, Pearson left in November 2011, to return to the Foxes.

Nick Barmby, November 2011–May 2012
P: 33   W: 13   D: 8   L: 12
The hometown hero was appointed caretaker manager following Pearson's departure. He took over the reins full-time in January 2012, but left only four months later.

Steve Bruce, June 2012–
Former Manchester United defender Steve Bruce was appointed to the Tigers hot seat in June 2012, the club and fans no doubt hoping he will emulate the promotion success he enjoyed when manager of Birmingham City.

IF THE CAP FITS ...

The grandly-named Edward Gordon Dundas Wright won his one and only full England cap in 1906 in a match against Wales – thus becoming the Tigers' first international. Wright also represented his country at the 1912 Olympics, held in Stockholm, Sweden, in which he was a Gold Medal winner with the national football team – another club first. He gained 20 caps for England at amateur level and, more than a century on, he is still the only Hull player to represent England while playing for the Tigers! At club level, he managed to captain City for seven consecutive seasons. Wright played as an outside-left and was known for having a great first touch. He had studied at Cambridge University and went on to teach Natural History and Science at Hymer's College. Later in his career he played for Leyton Orient and Portsmouth while also representing the famous Corinthians side with whom he toured with on two occasions in 1907. Wright left the UK in 1913 after accepting an offer of employment in South Africa working as a mining engineer and he stayed in the country for the remainder of his life.

NORWAY WE'LL BE INVITED BACK …

It is probably fair to say that the Norwegian representative of Trondheim & District who decided to arrange three friendlies in five days with the Tigers in 1912, probably didn't last too long in his job following the Tigers' departure. City striker Stan Fazackerley enjoyed his sojourn to the Fjords to such an extent there are rumours he returned in later life to build a small log cabin in order to reminisce about his exploits during the tour. In fact, Trondheim would have been better building a log cabin in front of their goal during their matches against City – they lost the first game 16–1, the second 15–1 but showed a vast improvement in their final game, only losing 9–0. Fazackerley bagged 11 goals in the first game, 4 in the second and 5 in the last to take his tally to 20 in 3 games! With 40 goals under their belts, City then took on IFK Gothenburg, playing them twice in three days and winning the games 1–0 and 4–0 before returning to England. The 10-day tour had yielded 5 wins and 45 goals with Fazackerley bagging 22 of them. Three days after their return, City were brought down to earth with a 7–4 home defeat to Everton – 'Faz' grabbing a hat-trick!

CLUB SPONSORS/SHIRT MANUFACTURERS

City have had 17 different sponsors since Hygena, the kitchen suppliers, became the first company to pay for the right to have their name on the Tigers' shirts. The name Bonus has featured most prominently, first as just Bonus between 1990 and 1993 and then Bonus Electrical who sponsored the kit from 2002 to 2007. IBC sponsored the shirt for four seasons, with University of Hull's brief deal (1997–99) sandwiched in between a couple of two-year stints. Eight companies have agreed just one-year sponsorships while Karoo and Kingston Communications uniquely have sponsored the home and away jerseys under separate deals since 2007.

When it comes to actually making the City shirts, there have been numerous deals over the 34 years since striking a deal with a sports company first came into being. Europa Sports ruled the roost from the mid-70s until 1980 when Adidas took over. The global giants made way for Admiral in 1982, who enjoyed an eight-year association. Match Winner and Super League dominated the 1990s with four years each. Umbro are the current shirt manufacturer and agreed a three-year deal with the club in 2007.

Season	Manufacturer	Sponsor
2012/13	Adidas	Cash Converters
2011/12	Adidas	Cash Converters
2010/11	Adidas	totesport.com
2009/10	Umbro	totesport.com
2008/09	Umbro	Karoo (Home)/ Kingston Comms (Away)
2007/08	Umbro	Karoo (Home)/ Kingston Comms (Away)
2006/07	Diadora	Bonus Electrical
2005/06	Diadora	Bonus Electrical
2004/05	Diadora	Bonus Electrical
2003/04	Patrick	Bonus Electrical
2002/03	Patrick	Bonus Electrical
2001/02	Patrick	Sportscard
2000/01	Avec	IBC
1999/2000	Avec	IBC
1998/99	SuperLeague	University of Hull

1997/98	SuperLeague	University of Hull
1996/97	SuperLeague	IBC
1995/96	Super League	IBC
1994/95	Pelada	Needler's Sweets
1993/94	Match Winner	Pepis
1992/93	Match Winner	Bonus
1991/92	Match Winner	Bonus
1990/91	Match Winner	Bonus
1989/90	Admiral	Dale Farm
1988/89	Admiral	Riding Bitter
1987/88	Admiral	Mansfield Beers
1986/87	Admiral	Twydale
1985/86	Admiral	Arrow Air
1984/85	Admiral	Arrow Air
1983/84	Admiral	Hygena
1982/83	Admiral	
1980–2	Adidas	
1975–80	Europa Sports	

WHEN CITY PUT THREE PAST BARCELONA …

For a mid-table Division Two side, the Tigers 1951 close-season tour of Spain makes impressive reading more than 50 years on. Having finished tenth in the League, City flew out to Madrid to begin their prestigious friendlies against Atletico Madrid. A crowd approaching 45,000 watched City humbled 4–0 by the reigning La Liga champions at the Estadio Metropolitano de Madrid, but the experience was unforgettable for all connected with Humberside. Next up was a trip to San Mames three days later to face Athletic Bilbao – a side that had the legendary forward line of Zarra, Panizo, Rafa Iriondo, Venancio and Agustín Gaínza. It looked like lambs to the slaughter on paper but City gave an excellent account of themselves, only losing 2–0 against a formidable outfit.

The jewel in the crown of this Spanish tour, however, was without doubt the trip to the Camp de Les Corts to face Copa del Rey champions Barcelona. In a fantastic match, two goals from Don Revie and another from Alf Ackerman saw the Tigers score three goals against one of the best teams in the world. The 25,000 home fans might have wondered who this plucky English side actually were prior to kick-off, but after securing a 5–3 win, it's safe to say the Catalonians went home talking about a brave Hull City side that had pushed their team all the way.

DEANO SAID IT…

'Some young footballers need to go out and earn £140 a week on a building site, then when they do earn money in football they will appreciate it.'

Deano's plan to keep players in the real world

'It is not an overnight thing. It has always intrigued me to watch a manager and see what they do.'

Deano's thoughts on management

'When I did it the response I got was phenomenal. I told a story from the heart and was honest. If people don't like it, and don't like me, then fair enough. I said it as it is. I've lost a few family members from it but that's just the way it is. I've got my own family now, my wife and kids to look after.'

Deano on his no-holds barred autobiography

'When I was on the building site and at Birds Eye it was tough times, tough times. But I always believed I was good enough. It got to the stage where I went on trial at places like Cambridge and York and Sunderland, but they never gave me a second glance. I thought, "Please someone, just give me a chance." I've been given that chance and I've never looked back since. I worked out that nothing was given to me on a plate and I've worked hard every day of my life. Now here I am reaping my rewards, playing for Hull City at Wembley in the last game of the season.

Deano – all good things come to he who waits!

TURNING JAPANESE?

Probably the only time the names Yamaguchi and Ogi will feature on City's scoresheet was back in August 1971 when the Tigers took on a touring Japan national team. More than 10,000 curious locals attended the pre-season friendly at Boothferry Park and apart from the two Japan own goals from the aforementioned players, Paul O'Riley, Ken Wagstaff and Ian Butler also scored in a comfortable 5–0 victory.

DO YOU KNOW YOUR ENEMY?

It's fair to say that, like a number of single-club cities, City have few serious rivals in the football world. There are geographical rivalries, including Scunthorpe United and Grimsby Town from across the Humber. Sadly, for locals who do enjoy a good ding-dong with the Mariners or the Iron, both clubs occupy lower positions on the football league ladder, therefore 'Humber Derbies' are a rarity in the region. The 2007/08 season, however, proved to be an exception with Scunthorpe and the Tigers both in the Championship; City completed a League double.

For many of the City faithful, their greatest rivals are Leeds United. This stems from the mid-1970s – a time of great success for the Lilywhites and a period of general mediocrity for City – when a lot of Leeds supporters were resident in the city. Grudge matches only returned in recent years when the two were pitted against each other in the second-tier of the Football League. It seems the Leeds fans do not reciprocate these feelings, even while they play their games in League One.

One rivalry with some meaning to it comes in the form of the Yorkshire derby with Sheffield United – the heated feeling towards the South Yorkshire club originates from the 1983/84 season when the Blades were promoted at Hull's expense after scoring more goals. The Tigers only managed two strikes on the final day of the season, when a third would have guaranteed elevation to the Second Division. Salt was rubbed into the wounds by the fact that the Blades' leading scorer was a former City striker in the guise of Keith Edwards!

TESTIMONIALS

Benefit games have, by and large, been few and far between over the years, with just nine in total. Club legend Chris Chilton easily commanded the biggest crowd, with just shy of 30,000 packing into Boothferry Park (swelled no doubt by one or two Leeds-loving locals). The next highest crowd is under half of Chilton's figure and the lowest was for Malcolm Lord, with under 2,000 bothering to show up. In order of attendance, here are the details:

Chris Chilton Testimonial v. Leeds United, May 1971
Attendance: 28,350
Score: 7–6
Scorers: Chilton (3), Wagstaff (3), McKechnie

Andy Davidson Testimonial v. Man City, April 1970
Attendance: 13,027
Score: 2–0
Scorers: Wagstaff (2)

Jimmy Lodge Testimonial v. Derby County, April 1970
Attendance: 8,937
Score: 2–2
Scorers: Houghton, Wagstaff

Gareth Roberts Testimonial v. Spurs, May 1992
Attendance: 9,994
Score: 2–6
Scorers: Whitehurst, Roberts (pen)

Neil Mann Testimonial v. Grimsby Town, July 2003
Attendance: 7,496
Score: 0–1
Scorers: N/A

Billy Bly Testimonial v. All Star XI, October 1961
Attendance: 5,387
Score: 4–3
Scorers: Mortensen, Moore (2), Harris

Billy Wilkinson Testimonial v. West Ham, May 1973
Attendance: 2,853
Score: 5–3
Scorers: Lord (2), Greenwood (2), Pearson

Jed Radcliffe Testimonial v. Spurs, April 1988
Attendance: 2,077
Score: 2–1
Scorers: Saville, de Mange

Malcolm Lord Testimonial v. Sunderland, May 1981
Attendance: 1,753
Score: 2–0
Scorers: Chilton, Edwards

ANGLO-ITALIAN CUP

The Tigers' foray into European football lasted just one season when, during the 1972/73 campaign, they took on teams from Italy in the much-maligned Anglo-Italian Cup. In fact, City did exceptionally well, beating Lazio 1–0 at Boothferry Park in February 1973 in front of 7,325 fans. Almost 5,000 spectators, including a smattering of Tigers fans, saw Fiorentina win the second group match 1–0 on Italian soil a month later before goals from Knighton and Houghton secured a 2–1 victory over Verona.

The trouble was, the other English teams in City's group were all doing well, too, with Crystal Palace, Manchester United and Luton Town all gaining impressive results against the Italians. A win away to Bari, who'd lost all three of their group games up to that point, would give City a great chance of making it to the semi-final stages, but Bari ground out a 0–0 draw and the opportunity was gone. For the record, Newcastle United beat Fiorentina 2–1 at Wembley Stadium to claim the trophy.

Total record:

Pld 4   W 2   D 1   L 1   F 3   A 2

HOP SCOTCH

City decided their 1991/92 pre-season tour should be kept as straightforward and cost-effective as possible. With this in mind, they arranged a three-match 'tour' of Scotland. With three matches to play in the space of five days, the main aim was to build up fitness prior to the League campaign and Terry Dolan's side made the perfect start with an impressive 4–2 win over Celtic at Parkhead. A 1–0 defeat to Ayr United followed just three days later but City signed off on a high with a 1–0 victory over Clydebank – a match that certainly captured the imagination of the locals of whom 471 turned up!

A LOAD OF BULL –
JIMMY BULLARDISMS ...

'The paperwork has been sorted and if Jurgen rang I'd definitely be interested. I used to play with England midfielder Frank Lampard at West Ham and the chance to face him in the World Cup would be too good to turn down.'

Jimmy ponders playing international football for Germany

'I've heard a lot of talk about wages and demands and all that I can honestly say is I don't play football for money.'

Is Bullard the last of a dying breed?

'I'm getting into designing and architecture at the minute. I've got one starting in the Algarve, all these modern designs and modern interiors and all that...I'm only new to it, it's my first one, but I've got some crazy ideas.'

Could Jimmy be the next Laurence Llewelyn-Bowen?

'I was a painter and decorator for two or three years, working 7 till 5 up town. I was lucky as my dad used to give me time off to rest before games which probably helped my game.'

Jimmy paints a picture of his early days

'I felt like Fulham didn't want me and it was as simple as that really. I was in talks with Fulham over a contract and I was told I'm not getting a new contract and I can leave in January. So for a player to be told that was quite harsh, you know, and I came up to speak to Hull and it was totally different, and it sort of made it a lot easier for me. I'm only human, I just wanted to play for a team who really wanted me, and Hull showed me that really.'

Jimmy on finding a new home on Humberside

'I've never been interested in money as such. So it's sheer football reasons. I wasn't asking for anything. I was in contract talks and the talks went as far as "we are not going to offer you any sort of contract." I left saying I wanted to play for a club who wants me. It was agreed like that. It was a weird discussion I had.'

Jimmy explains why he became a Tiger

'I don't go around trying to be funny, it just depends. The film was rubbish, I was bored. Everybody's done that, haven't they?'

Jimmy explains why he once threw sweets at a bald guy during a movie!

GROUNDS FOR CONCERN?

City have played at numerous venues over the years – here is a complete list:

The Boulevard

City's early matches were played at The Boulevard, the old home of Rugby League side Hull FC. On 1 September 1904, the Tigers' inaugural match took place against Notts County with an estimated 6,000 in attendance. The Tigers notched up an impressive start, holding the more experienced County to a 2–2 draw. After disputes with their rugby-playing landlords, City moved to Anlaby Road Cricket Ground just a year later.

The club returned to The Boulevard in 1944/45 when City's Anlaby Road home suffered serious damage from bombings in the Second World War. Rugby League was still played there and it hosted four Rugby League World Cup matches until the council decided to close it in 2005. The Boulevard was re-opened in October 2007 for the purposes of greyhound racing, but after just eight meetings, the stadium returned to being used for amateur rugby games.

The Cricket Circle
Home to City for a mere 17 games – a stop-gap home in effect – before the Tigers could move into their purpose-built stadium at Anlaby Road.

Anlaby Road
The ground was opened 24 March 1906 when the Tigers faced Blackpool in a match that finished 2–2. From this point the stadium was continuously updated, with extra seats and roofing being added for the next decade. Disaster struck on Easter Monday 1914, however, when a fire turned the main stand into ashes. The cause was never discovered, and a replacement stand was soon built after funding was given by club director Bob Mungall.

Anlaby Road suffered damage – as did the rest of the city – in air raids from the German Luftwaffe and the club decided that it was not economically viable to carry out the repair works and so decided against continuing with their tenancy at the venue. Amateur football continued to be played there in the years after with the final match taking place on 26 April 1965 – thereafter the stadium was subsequently demolished in order to make way for a section of railway track.

Boothferry Park
Construction during the Second World War and the years after was a complicated and risky industry due to the lack of materials available caused by shortages and threat of further bomb damage. Boothferry Park initially had one stand and to save money, turnstiles and other

fixtures from the Anlaby Road site were put in place at the new site. By 1949 the ground could hold more than 55,000 spectators, something which it succeeded in doing on 26 February that year, when the club hosted Manchester United, creating a record attendance that still stands today.

Many fans enjoyed watching the matches from 'Bunkers Hill' which was the terracing at the South Stand end, until it's renovation in 1964 which also involved the building of a gym at the back of the stadium. The leisure centre still stands today, and is frequently used for a variety of sporting events.

Floodlights were installed in 1953 for the first time at Boothferry Park, but due to their low quality, they had to be replaced within the space of a decade. The mid-1980s saw an overhaul of the facilities after an inspection of the stadium deemed that certain aspects of the ground made it unsafe for the public to watch sporting events safely there. During this period the capacity had to be reduced and, in turn the Boothferry Park was modernised.

The infamous and temporary East Stand covering was a cause for concern for many years, and eventually that side of the ground had to be closed in 1996 due to safety issues. For many, Boothferry Park became a representation of the plethora of problems that the club suffered in the late 1990s, and caused much controversy as it was not included in the package in which the club was sold in 1997. The previous owner, David Lloyd, was still the registered landlord, which resulted in the team being locked out of their home on numerous occasions – that is until the Tigers moved to the state-of-the-art KC Stadium.

Kingston Communications Stadium (KC Stadium)

At a cost of £43.5m, Hull City Council and local company Kingston Communications built a new stadium for Hull City FC and the Rugby League outfit Hull FC. With a capacity of 25,000, the new venue spent its first couple of seasons looking somewhat out of place in the lower reaches of the Football League. City began their residency in the new stadium in 2002, and it has been their home ever since, taking in three promotions in its short life and proving something of a talisman in the club's history. In 2006 it was voted the 'Best Ground' at the Football League awards and in 2008 it enjoyed its first full campaign of Premier League fixtures. With the Tigers residing in the Championship (at the time of writing), the KC Stadium nonetheless remains worthy of top-flight football.

TIGERS' COMPLETE FA CUP RECORD

Starting from the present and working back, here is City's record in the world's most prestigious domestic tournament – the Football Association Cup:

Date	Round	Venue	Opposition	Result
2011/12				
7/1/12	3	H	Ipswich Town	3–1 W
28/1/12	4	H	Crawley Town	0–1 L
2010/11				
8/1/11	3	H	Wigan Athletic	2–3 L
2009/10				
2/1/10	3	A	Wigan Athletic	1–4 L
2008/09				
3/1/09	3	H	Newcastle United	0–0 D
14/1/09	3R	A	Newcastle United	1–0 W
24/1/09	4	H	Millwall	2–0 W
14/2/09	5	A	Sheffield United	1–1 W
26/2/09	5R	H	Sheffield United	2–1 W
17/3/09	6	A	Arsenal	1–2 L

Date	Round	Venue	Opposition	Result
2007/08				
5/1/08	3	A	Plymouth Argyle	2–3 L
2006/07				
6/1/07	3	H	Middlesbrough	1–1D
16/1/07	3R	A	Middlesbrough	3–4 L
2005/06				
7/1/06	3	H	Aston Villa	0–1 L
2004/05				
13/11/04	1	H	Morecambe	3–2 W
4/12/04	2	H	Macclesfield	4–0 W
8/1/05	3	H	Colchester	0–2 L
2003/04				
8/11/03	1	A	Cheltenham Town	1–3 L
2002/03				
16/11/02	1	H	Macclesfield Town	0–3 L
2001/02				
17/11/01	1	A	Northwich Victoria	5–2 W
8/12/01	2	H	Oldham Athletic	2–3 L
2000/01				
18/11/00	1	A	Kettering Town	0–0 D
28/11/00	1R	H	Kettering Town	0–1 L
1999/2000				
29/10/99	1	A	Macclesfield Town	0–0 D
9/11/99	1R	H	Macclesfield Town	4–0 W
20/11/99	2	A	Hayes	2–2 D
30/11/99	2R	H	Hayes	3–2 (aet) W
11/12/99	3	H	Chelsea	1–6 L

Date	Round	Venue	Opposition	Result
1998/99				
14/11/98	1	A	Salisbury City	2–0 W
5/12/98	2	A	Luton Town	2–1 W
2/1/99	3	A	Aston Villa	0–3 L
1997/98				
15/11/97	1	H	Hednesford Town	0–2 L
1996/97				
17/11/96	1	N	Whitby Town	0–0 D
26/11/96	1R	H	Whitby Town	8–4 (aet) W
7/12/96	2	H	Crewe Alexandra	1–5 L
1995/96				
11/11/95	1	H	Wrexham	0–0 D
21/11/95	1R	A	Wrexham	0–0 D
				(but lost 3–1 on pens)
1994/95				
12/11/94	1	H	Lincoln City	0–1 L
1993/94				
23/11/93	1	N	Runcorn	2–0 W
4/12/93	2	A	Chester City	0–2 L
1992/93				
14/11/92	1	A	Darlington	2–1 W
5/12/92	2	A	Rotherham United	0–1 L
1991/92				
16/11/91	1	A	Morecambe	1–0 W
7/12/91	2	A	Blackpool	1–0 W
4/1/92	3	H	Chelsea	0–2 L

Date	Round	Venue	Opposition	Result
1990/91				
5/1/91	3	H	Notts County	2–5 L
1989/90				
6/1/90	3	H	Newcastle United	0–1 L
1988/89				
7/1/89	3	A	Cardiff City	2–1 W
28/1/89	4	A	Bradford City	2–1 W
18/2/89	5	H	Liverpool	2–3 L
1987/88				
9/1/88	3	A	Watford	1–1 D
12/1/88	3 R	H	Watford	2–2 (aet) D
18/1/88	3R2	A	Watford	0–1 L
1986/87				
31/1/87	3	A	Shrewsbury Town	2–1 W
3/2/87	4	A	Swansea City	1–0 W
21/2/87	5	A	Wigan Athletic	0–3 L
1985/86				
7/1/86	3	A	Plymouth Argyle	1–0
25/1/86	4	H	Brighton & HA	2–3 L
1984/85				
17/11/84	1	H	Bolton Wanderers	2–1 W
8/12/84	2	A	Tranmere Rovers	3–0 W
5/1/85	3	A	Brighton & HA	0–1 L
1983/84				
19/11/83	1	A	Penrith	2–0 W
10/12/83	2	A	Rotherham United	1–2 L

Date	Round	Venue	Opposition	Result
1982/83				
20/11/82	1	H	Sheffield United	1–1 D
23/11/82	1R	A	Sheffield United	0–2 L
1981/82				
21/11/81	1	A	Rochdale	1–1 D
24/11/81	1R	H	Rochdale	2–2 (aet) D
30/11/81	1R2	N	Rochdale	1–0 (aet) W
4/1/82	2	H	Hartlepool United	2–0 W
18/1/82	3	A	Chelsea	0–0 D
21/1/82	3R	H	Chelsea	0–2 L
1980/81				
22/11/80	1	H	Halifax Town	2–1 W
13/12/80	2	H	Blyth Spartans	1–1 D
15/12/80	2R	A	Blyth Spartans	2–2 (aet) D
22/12/80	2R2	H	Blyth Spartans	2–1 (aet) W
3/1/81	3	H	Doncaster Rovers	1–0 W
24/1/81	4	A	Tottenham Hotspur	0–2 L
1979/80				
24/11/79	1	A	Carlisle United	3–3 D
28/11/79	1R	H	Carlisle United	0–2 L
1978/79				
25/11/78	1	H	Stafford Rangers	2–1 W
16/12/78	2	A	Carlisle United	0–3 L
1977/78				
7/1/78	3	H	Leicester City	0–1 L
1976/77				
8/1/77	3	H	Port Vale	1–1 D
10/1/77	3R	A	Port Vale	1–3 (aet) L

Date	Round	Venue	Opposition	Result
1975/76				
3/1/76	3	H	Plymouth Argyle	1–1 D
6/1/76	3R	A	Plymouth Argyle	4–1 W
2/2/76	4	A	Sunderland	0–1 L
1974/75				
4/1/75	3	A	Fulham	1–1 D
7/1/75	3R	H	Fulham	2–2 (aet) D
13/1/75	3R2	N	Fulham	0–1
1973/74				
5/1/74	3	A	Bristol City	1–1 D
8/1/74	3R	H	Bristol City	0–1 L
1972/73				
13/1/73	3	A	Stockport County	0–0 D
23/1/73	3R	H	Stockport County	2–0 (aet) W
3/2/73	4	H	West Ham	1–0 W
24/2/73	5	A	Coventry City	0–3 L
1971/72				
15/1/72	3	A	Norwich City	3–0 W
9/2/72	4	A	Coventry City	1–0 W
26/2/72	5	A	Stoke City	1–4 L
1970/71				
2/1/71	3	H	Charlton Athletic	3–0 W
23/1/71	4	H	Blackpool	2–0 W
13/2/71	5	H	Brentford	2–1 W
6/3/71	6	H	Stoke City	2–3 L
1969/70				
3/1/70	3	H	Man City	0–1 L

Date	Round	Venue	Opposition	Result
1968/69				
4/1/69	3	H	Wolves	1–3 L
1967/68				
27/1/68	3	H	Middlesbrough	1–1 D
31/1/68	3R	A	Middlesbrough	2–2 (aet) D
7/2/68	3R2	N	Middlesbrough	0–1 L
1966/67				
28/1/67	3	H	Portsmouth	1–1 D
01/2/67	3R	A	Portsmouth	2–2 (aet) D
6/2/67	3R2	N	Portsmouth	1–3 L
1965/66				
13/11/65	1	A	Bradford Park Avenue	3–2 W
8/12/65	2	A	Gateshead	4–0 W
22/1/66	3	H	Southampton	1–0 W
12/2/66	4	H	Nottingham Forest	2–0 W
5/3/66	5	H	Southport	2–0 W
26/3/66	6	A	Chelsea	2–2 D
31/3/66	6R	H	Chelsea	1–3 L
1964/65				
14/11/64	1	A	Kidderminster H	4–1 W
5/12/64	2	H	Lincoln City	1–1 D
9/12/64	2R	A	Lincoln City	1–3 L
1963/64				
16/11/63	1	H	Crewe Alexandra	2–2 D
20/11/63	1R	A	Crewe Alexandra	3–1 W
7/12/63	2	A	Wrexham	3–0 W
4/1/64	3	H	Everton	1–1 D
7/1/64	3R	A	Everton	1–2 L

Date	Round	Venue	Opposition	Result
1962/63				
3/11/62	1	H	Crook Town	5–4 W
24/11/62	2	H	Workington Town	2–0 W
11/2/63	3	A	Leyton Orient	1–1 D
19/2/63	3R	H	Leyton Orient	0–2 (aet) L
1961/62				
4/11/61	1	H	Rhyl	1–0 W
25/11/61	2	H	Bradford City	0–2 L
1960/61				
5/11/60	1	H	Sutton Town	3–0 W
26/11/60	2	A	Darlington	1–1 D
28/11/60	2R	H	Darlington	1–1 (aet) D
12/12/60	2R2	A	Darlington	0–0 (aet) D
15/12/60	2R3	N	Darlington	3–0 W
7/1/61	3	H	Bolton Wanderers	0–1 L
1959/60				
9/1/60	3	A	Fulham	0–5 L
1958/59				
15/11/58	1	H	Stockport County	0–1 L
1957/58				
16/11/57	1	H	Crewe Alexandra	2–1 W
7/12/57	2	A	Port Vale	2–2 D
9/12/57	2R	H	Port Vale	4–3 (aet) W
4/1/58	3	H	Barnsley	1–1 D
8/1/58	3R	A	Barnsley	2–0 W
29/1/58	4	A	Sheffield Wednesday	3–4 L

Date	Round	Venue	Opposition	Result
1956/57				
17/11/56	1	H	Gateshead	4–0 W
8/12/56	2	H	York City	2–1 W
5/1/57	3	H	Bristol Rovers	3–4 L
1955/56				
7/1/56	3	A	Aston Villa	1–1 D
12/1/56	3R	H	Aston Villa	1–2 L
1954/55				
8/1/55	3	H	Birmingham City	0–2 L
1953/54				
9/1/54	3	A	Brentford	1–1 D
14/1/54	3R	H	Brentford	2–2 (aet) D
18/1/54	3R2	N	Brentford	5–2 W
30/1/54	4	A	Blackburn Rovers	2–2 D
4/2/54	4R	H	Blackburn Rovers	2–1 W
20/2/54	5	H	Tottenham Hotspur	1–1 D
24/2/54	5R	A	Tottenham Hotspur	0–2 L
1952/53				
10/1/53	3	H	Charlton Athletic	3–1 W
31/1/53	4	H	Gateshead	1–2 L
1951/52				
12/1/52	3	A	Manchester United	2–0 W
2/2/52	4	A	Blackburn Rovers	0–2 L
1950/51				
6/1/51	3	H	Everton	2–0 W
27/1/51	4	H	Rotherham United	2–0 W
10/2/51	5	A	Blackburn Rovers	0–3 L

Date	Round	Venue	Opposition	Result
1949/50				
7/1/50	3	A	Southport	0–0 D
12/1/50	3R	H	Southport	5–0 W
28/1/50	4	A	Stockport County	0–0 D
2/2/50	4R	H	Stockport County	0–2 L
1948/49				
27/11/48	1	H	Accrington Stanley	3–1 W
11/12/48	2	H	Reading	0–0 D
18/12/48	2	A	Reading	2–1 W
8/1/49	3	H	Blackburn Rovers	2–1 W
29/1/49	4	A	Grimsby Town	3–2 W
12/2/49	5	A	Stoke City	2–0 W
26/2/49	6	H	Manchester United	0–1 L
1947/48				
29/11/47	1	H	Southport	1–1 D
6/12/47	1R	A	Southport	3–2 W
13/12/47	2	H	Cheltenham Town	4–2 W
10/1/48	3	H	Middlesbrough	1–3 L
1946/47				
30/11/46	1	H	New Brighton	0–0 D
4/12/46	1R	A	New Brighton	2–1 (aet) W
14/12/46	2	A	Darlington	2–1 W
11/1/47	3	A	Blackburn Rovers	1–1 D
16/1/47	3R	H	Blackburn Rovers	0–3 L
1938/39				
26/11/38	1	H	Rotherham United	4–1 W
10/12/38	2	A	Chester	2–2 D
15/12/38	2R	H	Chester	0–1 L

Date	Round	Venue	Opposition	Result
1937/38				
27/11/37	1	H	Scunthorpe	4–0 W
11/12/37	2	A	Exeter City	2–1 W
8/1/38	3	A	Huddersfield Town	1–3 L
1936/37				
28/11/36	1	A	York City	2–5 L
1935/36				
11/1/36	3	A	West Bromwich Albion	0–2 L
1934/35				
12/1/35	3	A	Newcastle United	1–5 L
1933/34				
13/1/34	3	H	Brentford	1–0 W
27/1/34	4	H	Man City	2–2 D
31/1/34	4R	A	Man City	1–4 L
1932/33				
26/11/32	1	A	Stalybridge Celtic	8–2 W
10/12/32	2	A	Carlisle United	1–1 D
15/12/32	2	H	Carlisle United	2–1 W
14/1/33	3	H	Sunderland	0–2 L
1931/32				
28/11/31	1	H	Mansfield Town	4–1 W
12/12/31	2	A	New Brighton	4–0 W
9/1/32	3	A	Stoke City	0–3 L
1930/31				
10/1/31	3	H	Blackpool	1–2 L

Date	Round	Venue	Opposition	Result
1929/30				
11/1/30	3	A	Plymouth Argyle	4–3 W
25/1/30	4	H	Blackpool	3–1 W
15/2/30	5	A	Manchester City	2–1 W
1/3/30	6	A	Newcastle United	1–1 D
6/3/30	6R	H	Newcastle United	1–0 W
22/3/30	S/F	N	Arsenal	2–2 D
26/3/30	S/FR	N	Arsenal	0–1 L
1928/29				
12/1/29	3	H	Bradford Park Avenue	1–1 D
16/1/29	3R	A	Bradford Park Avenue	1–3 L
1927/28				
14/1/28	3	H	Leicester City	0–1 L
1926/27				
8/1/27	3	H	West Bromwich Albion	2–1 W
29/1/27	4	H	Everton	1–1 D
2/2/27	4R	A	Everton	2–2 D
7/2/27	4R2	N	Everton	3–2 W
19/2/27	5	A	Wolves	0–1 L
1925/26				
9/1/26	1	H	Aston Villa	0–3 L
1924/25				
10/1/25	1	H	Wolves	1–1 D
15/1/25	1R	A	Wolves	1–0 W
31/1/25	2	H	Crystal Palace	3–2 W
21/2/25	3	H	Leicester City	1–1 D
26/2/25	3R	A	Leicester City	1–3 L

Date	Round	Venue	Opposition	Result
1923/24				
12/1/24	1	H	Bolton Wanderers	1–1 D
16/1/24	1R	A	Bolton Wanderers	0–4 L
1922/23				
13/1/23	1	H	West Ham United	2–3 L
1921/22				
7/1/22	1q	H	Middlesbrough	5–0 W
28/1/22	2q	A	Nottingham Forest	0–3 W
8/1/22	1	H	Bath City	3–0 W
28/1/22	2	A	Crystal Palace	2–0 W
19/2/22	3	H	Burnley	3–0 W
5/3/22	4	H	Preston North End	0–0 D
10/3/22	4R	A	Preston North End	0–1 L
1920/21				
14/1/21	1	A	Sunderland	2–6 L
1914/15				
9/1/15	1	H	West Bromwich Albion	1–0 W
30/1/15	2	H	Northampton Town	2–1 W
20/2/15	3	A	Southampton	2–2 D
27/2/15	3R	H	Southampton	4–0 W
6/3/15	4	A	Bolton Wanderers	4–2 W
1913/14				
10/1/14	1	H	Bury	0–0 D
14/1/14	1R	A	Bury	1–2 L
1912/13				
11/1/13	1	A	Fulham	2–0 W
01/2/13	2	H	Newcastle United	0–0 D
5/2/13	2R	A	Newcastle United	0–3 L

Date	Round	Venue	Opposition	Result
1911/12				
13/1/12	1	A	Oldham Athletic	1–1 D
16/1/12	1R	H	Oldham Athletic	0–1 L
1910/11				
14/1/11	1	A	Bristol Rovers	0–0 D
19/1/11	1R	H	Bristol Rovers	1–0 W
4/2/11	2	H	Oldham Athletic	1–0 W
25/2/11	3	A	Newcastle United	2–3 L
1909/10				
15/1/10	1	A	Chelsea	1–2 L
1908/09				
16/1/09	1	H	Chelsea	1–1 D
20/1/09	1R	A	Chelsea	0–1 L
1907/08				
11/1/08	1	A	Woolwich Arsenal	0–0 D
16/1/08	1R	H	Woolwich Arsenal	4–1 W
01/2/08	2	H	Aston Villa	0–3 L
1906/07				
12/1/07	1	A	Tottenham Hotspur	0–0 D
17/1/07	1R	H	Tottenham Hotspur	0–0 (aet) D
21/1/07	1R2	A	Tottenham Hotspur	0–1 L
1905/06				
13/1/06	1	H	Reading	0–1 L

CAN YOU HEAR US ON THE BOX?

Here is a selection of City songs, old and new:

(To the tune of 'Que Sera, Sera')
Jim Bullard, Bullard
He's better than Steve Gerrard
He's thinner than Frank Lampard
Jim Bullard, Bullard

We love you City, we do
We love you City, we do
We love you City, we do
Oh City we love you

(Sung to 'Can't Help Falling In Love')
Wise men say only fools rush in
But I can't help falling in love with you
Take my hand, take my whole life too
For I can't help falling in love with you
The Tigers!

E I E I E I O
Up the Football League we go
When we win promotion
This is what we'll sing
We all love you
We all love you
Browny is our king

(Sung to the tune of 'Jingle Bells' at away games)
Jingle bells, jingle bells, jingle all the way
Oh, what fun it is to see Hull City win away

(Sung to the tune of 'H A P P Y')
City 'til I die
I'm City 'til I die
I know I am
I'm sure I am
I'm City 'til I die

(Sung to the tune of 'Guantanamera')
Mauled by the Tigers
You're being mauled by the Tigers
Mauled by the Tigers
You're being mauled by the Tigers

(Sung to the tune of 'Yellow Submarine')
In the town where I was born
There's a football team called Hull City (Hull City!)
And we make the pilgrimage
Every Saturday to Boothferry (2, 3, 4)
We all follow a black and amber team
A black and amber team
A black and amber team

(Sung to the chorus of 'Can't Take My Eyes Off You')
Oh Ian Ashbee, he's neither here nor there
Oh Ian Ashbee, he's f***ing everywhere
Oh Ian Ashbee, Ashbee's gonna get you

From Boothferry to Wem-ber-ley
We'll keep the Hull flag flying high
Flying high
Up in the sky
We'll keep the Hull flag flying high
From Boothferry to Wem-ber-ley
We'll keep the Hull flag flying high

(Sung to the tune of 'Our House')
Myhill in the middle of our goal

(Sung to the tune of *The Addams' Family* theme)
His name is Geovanni
He is Braziliani
He's part of City's army
He's gonna keep us up

(Sung to the tune of 'Always Look On The Bright Side
Of Life')
Always s*** on the south side of the bridge

Give us a
C (C)
I (I)
T (T)
Y. . . (Y. . .)
And what have you got?!
City/the Tigers. . . .

(Sung to the tune of 'The Wild Rover')
And it's Hull City
Hull City AFC
We're by far the greatest team
The world has ever seen

(Sung loosely to the tune of 'Sloop John B' at away
games)
I don't wanna go home
I don't wanna go ho-o-ome
This is the best trip I've ever been on

We're the left side, we're the left side, we're the left side,
Hull City
We're the right side, we're the right side, we're the right
side, Hull City

(Sung to the tune of 'Tom Hark')
Silverware, we don't care
We follow City everywhere

HERO TO ZERO …

Colin Appleton holds the record of best and worst
record as Hull City manager. His first spell as Tigers'
boss was from August 1982 to May 1984 and during
that time, City had a win ratio of 51.9 per cent from
his 104 games in charge. After failing to take his team
up by the narrowest of margins during the 1983/84
campaign, Appleton quit Boothferry Park and moved
on to pastures new. Appleton proved the old adage 'you
should never go back' to be true when he returned as
Tigers boss in 1989. His second spell lasted just over two
months in which City won just one of their opening 16
games – a win ratio of 6.3 per cent. Appleton was duly
sacked, though supporters still remember his first spell
with fondness.

ASH SAID IT …

'Hull is close to my heart and I've been looked after by
the club. I'll be immensely proud to lead the team out at
Wembley. Some people don't get the chance to do that
but I've got the chance now to lead them into the Premier
League. It means more to me because of what I've come
through and I've got a lot of people to thank for that.'

The Tigers' skipper, prior to the 2007/08 play-off final

'I wasn't thinking about not playing again at that point.
I was thinking about not being able to go down to the
park with my kids and stuff like that. That's how serious

it was, but we were lucky enough that the bone had not come away and we just drilled the holes and luckily enough it grew back.'

Ash's initial reaction to being diagnosed with a rare bone condition

'I watched bits and bobs from Europe last week – mainly from the Chelsea game. Wouldn't it be great? Leading Hull out at Roma? It would not be so much the icing on the cake as the hundreds and thousands on top of that.'

Ash reveals his *Boy's Own* dream

'If you had asked me five years ago when I was leading the side out against Lincoln if we would be playing against Manchester United and Chelsea in a few years' time, I would have said no. So Europe is something I would never say no to.'

Nor would any other Tigers fan, Ash!

THE FIRST GAME ...

City's first ever League fixture was on 2 September 1905 when Barnsley were the visitors to the Anlaby Road ground. Approximately 8,000 people saw the Tigers announce their arrival in style, winning 4–1 with two goals from Gordon and further strikes from Spence and Wilson giving Ambrose Langley's team the perfect start.

DEANO SAID IT – MORE WINDASS PEARLERS ...

'There have been plenty of times when I have embarrassed myself, and let myself get wound up when I shouldn't. Though if you'd heard the dog's abuse I get. . . .'

'I've always had a drink after a game on a Saturday. Win, lose or draw, it's a release, my way of getting it out of my system. I get drunk if necessary. But then I take my lads to play their own football on the Sunday, and start preparing for the next game.'

'I try hard, and I'm not lazy, but I'm the worst bloody footballer in the world out there. Like Dean Saunders used to say, a lot of players look brilliant in training, but don't do it in matches. There are match players and there are training-ground players, and it's all about mental strength.'

'I don't think I've ever gone more than five games without scoring, and a manager who picks me knows what he is going to get. He knows I'm not going to go past two or three defenders and smash it into the top corner, but if there's a ball into the box on to my head, I might miss the first but I'll get the bloody second.'

'I've been one of those players who has been slaughtered by some managers, really bollocked, had teacups thrown at me, the whole works. Usually I take it, but sometimes I've had a little argue back. I've also had managers who take the opposite approach. I've never really minded which, because I try just as hard whatever.'

FINAL DAY TIGERS

City generally fare quite well on the final day of the League season, losing only one in three of their closing matches on average (not including play-off games). The Tigers lost their very first final day fixture (stay with us) against Lincoln City in 1906 and it wasn't until 1910 that they suffered another loss in the ultimate game of the season, going down 3–0 at Oldham Athletic. In fact,

Barnsley were the only other team to beat City in this fixture until Port Vale won 2–1 in 1924, meaning that from 1906 until 1923, the Tigers only lost two of their final 14 last-day clashes. The biggest last day win was a 5–0 victory over Wrexham in 1932 and the worst ending to a campaign was a 5–0 reverse at Oldham Athletic in 1928.

The total record is:

P 97   W 43   D 20   L 34

ABANDONED!

City have taken part in eight games that have had to be abandoned due to one reason or another. The first match to be called to a halt was against Leeds City in 1905 when the referee decided 50 minutes play was enough. The score was 0–0 at the time and the rearranged game ended 1–1. Two years later the FA Cup first round replay with Tottenham was abandoned with the score at 0–0 and 100 minutes on the clock. Sense prevailed and the result stood due to the fact a replay was needed anyway – Spurs won the re-match 1–0. Several years passed before proceedings were stopped again, with bad light forcing City and Glossop to meet again later in the 1912/13 campaign. The Tigers won the fixture 2–0 at Anlaby Road after the original had prematurely ended goalless. Bad light also stopped play with City leading Oldham 1–0 at Boundary Park and just five minutes remaining. The re-match ended 0–0 but fortunately the lost point didn't stop the Tigers winning the 1948/49 Division Three (North) title. It seemed like fog had saved City from a pummelling when the match with Bury was called to a halt at Gigg Lane in 1954. City were 4–1 down with 75 minutes gone, though sadly Bury still comfortably won the re-arranged game 3–0 – this is the only time a game in which City actually conceded goals has been abandoned. Heavy snow forced the teams off Boothferry Park with the score still 0–0 and 45 minutes played against Swindon Town in 1963. The rearranged fixture also ended all-square, 1–1. In 1971, the Tigers raced into a 2–0 half-time lead against Blackburn Rovers only for heavy fog off the Humber to scupper the result and Rovers claimed a 0–0 draw in the re-match. The last game to fail to reach its conclusion involving the Tigers was back in November 1994 when the FA Cup clash with Runcorn was called off, though City did win the replayed game 2–0.

Total record for games abandoned:

P	W	D	L	F	A
8	2	5	1	4	4

Total record for rearranged games:

P	W	D	L	F	A
8	2	4	2	7	7

WE'VE ARRIVED!

A measure of City's progress was the invitation to join the prestigious 2009/10 Asia Trophy in Beijing. The Tigers met Chinese outfit Beijing Guoan in the semi-final, winning 5–4 on penalties after a 1–1 draw. City then played Tottenham in the final after Spurs had knocked out West Ham 1–0 in the other semi. Unfortunately, Spurs beat City 3–0. Ironically, the tournament fell in what would eventually become the Chinese Year of the Tiger!

City chairman Paul Duffen commented after the announcement of Hull's participation: 'To go out there with Tottenham and West Ham and playing at the Workers stadium is understandably a huge moment for the club.'

It proves the Tigers have come a long way in a short space of time – one of the Tigers' 2008/09 friendlies was against – no disrespect – North Ferriby United!

COMPLETE LEAGUE CUP HISTORY

Date	Round	Venue	Opposition	Result
2011/12				
9/8/11	1	H	Macclesfield	0–2 L
2010/11				
24/8/10	2	A	Brentford	2–1 L
2009/10				
25/8/09	2	H	Southend	3–1 W
23/9/09	3	H	Everton	0–4 L
2008/09				
26/8/08	2	A	Swansea City	1–2 (aet) L
2007/08				
15/8/07	1	A	Crewe Alexandra	3–0 W
28/8/07	2	A	Wigan Athletic	1–0 W
26/9/07	3	H	Chelsea	0–4 L
2006/07				
22/08/06	1	H	Tranmere Rovers	2–1 (aet) W
19/9/06	2	H	Hartlepool	0–0 D
			(Won 3–2 on penalties)	
24/10/06	3	A	Watford	1–2 L
2005/06				
23/8/05	1	A	Blackpool	1–2 L
2004/05				
24/8/04	1	H	Wrexham	2–2 D
			(Lost 3–1 on pens)	
2003/04				
23/8/03	1	A	Wigan Athletic	0–2 L

Date	Round	Venue	Opposition	Result
2002/03				
10/9/02	1	H	Leicester	2–4 L
2001/02				
21/8/01	1	A	Wrexham	3–2 W
12/9/01	2	A	Derby County	0–3 L
2000/01				
5/9/00	1	A	Notts County	0–2 L
1999/2000				
10/8/99	1(L1)	A	Rotherham United	1–0 W
24/8/99	1(L2)	H	Rotherham United	2–0 W
			(Won 3–0 on agg)	
14/9/99	2(L1)	H	Liverpool	1–5 L
21/9/99	2(L2)	A	Liverpool	2–4 L
			(Lost 9–3 on agg)	
1998/99				
11/8/98	1(L1)	A	Stockport County	2–2 D
18/8/98	1(L2)	H	Stockport County	0–0 D
			(Agg 2–2, won on away goals)	
15/9/98	2(L1)	A	Bolton Wanderers	1–3 L
22/9/98	2(L2)	H	Bolton Wanderers	2–3 L
			(Lost 6–3 on agg)	
1997/98				
12/8/97	1(L1)	A	Macclesfield Town	0–0 D
26/8/97	1(L2)	H	Macclesfield Town	2–1 (aet) W
			(Won 2–1 on agg)	
16/9/97	2(L1)	H	Crystal Palace	1–0 W
30/9/97	2(L2)	A	Crystal Palace	1–2 L
			(2–2 on agg, won on away goals)	
15/10/97	3	A	Newcastle United	0–2 L

Date	Round	Venue	Opposition	Result
1996/97				
20/8/96	1(L1)	H	Scarborough	2–2 D
3/9/96	1(L2)	A	Scarborough	2–3 L
				(Lost 5–4 on agg)
1995/96				
15/8/95	1(L1)	H	Carlisle United	1–2 L
22/8/95	1(L2)	A	Carlisle United	4–2 W
				(Won 5–4 on agg)
20/9/95	2(L1)	A	Coventry City	0–2 L
4/10/95	2(L2)	H	Coventry City	0–1 L
				(Lost 3–0 on agg)
1994/95				
16/8/94	1(L1)	H	Scarborough	2–1 W
23/8/94	1(L2)	A	Scarborough	0–2 L
				(Lost 3–2 on agg)
1993/94				
16/8/93	1(L1)	A	Notts County	0–2 L
23/8/93	1(L2)	H	Notts County	3–1 W
			(3–3 on agg, lost on away goals)	
1992/93				
18/8/92	1(L1)	H	Rotherham United	2–2 D
25/8/92	1(L2)	A	Rotherham United	0–1 L
				(Lost 3–2 on agg)
1991/92				
20/8/91	1(L1)	A	Blackburn Rovers	1–1 D
27/8/91	1(L2)	H	Blackburn Rovers	1–0 W
				(Won 2–1 on agg)
24/9/91	2(L1)	A	QPR	0–3 L
9/10/91	2(L2)	H	QPR	1–5 L
				(Lost 8–1 on agg)

Date	Round	Venue	Opposition	Result
1990/91				
25/9/90	2(L1)	H	Wolves	0–0 D
9/10/90	2(L2)	A	Wolves	1–1 D
				(Won on away goals)
25/10/90	3	A	Coventry City	0–3 L
1989/90				
22/9/89	1(L1)	H	Grimsby Town	1–0 W
19/9/89	1(L2)	A	Grimsby Town	0–2 L
				(Lost 2–1 on agg)
1988/89				
28/9/88	2(L1)	A	Arsenal	0–3 L
12/10/88	2(L2)	H	Arsenal	1–2 L
				(Lost 5–1 on agg)
1987/88				
23/9/87	2(L1)	A	Manchester United	0–5 L
7/10/87	2(L2)	H	Manchester United	0–1 L
				(Lost 6–0 on agg)
1986/87				
23/9/86	2(L1)	H	Grimsby Town	1–0 W
7/10/86	2(L1)	A	Grimsby Town	1–1 D
				(Won 2–1 on agg)
28/10/86	3	A	Shrewsbury Town	0–1 L
1985/86				
20/8/85	1(L1)	A	Halifax Town	1–1 D
3/9/85	1(L2)	H	Halifax Town	3–0 W
				(Won 4–1 on agg)
24/9/85	2(L1)	A	QPR	0–3 L
8/10/85	2(L2)	H	QPR	1–5 L
				(Lost 8–1 on agg)

Date	Round	Venue	Opposition	Result
1984/85				
29/8/84	1(L1)	A	Lincoln City	2–0 W
4/9/84	1(L2)	H	Lincoln City	4–1 W
				(Won 6–1 on agg)
25/9/84	2(L1)	A	Southampton	2–3 L
9/10/84	2(L2)	H	Southampton	2–2 D
				(Lost 5–4 on agg)
1983/84				
30/8/83	1(L1)	H	Lincoln City	0–0 D
14/9/83	1(L2)	A	Lincoln City	1–3 L
				(Lost 3–1 on agg)
1982/83				
31/8/82	1(L1)	A	Sheffield United	1–3 L
14/9/82	1(L2)	H	Sheffield United	1–0 W
				(Lost 3–2 on agg)
1981/82				
2/9/81	1(L1)	A	Lincoln City	0–3 L
15/9/81	1(L2)	H	Lincoln City	1–1 D
				(Lost 4–1 on agg)
1980/81				
9/8/80	1(L1)	A	Lincoln City	0–5 L
12/8/80	1(L2)	H	Lincoln City	0–2 L
				(Lost 7–0 on agg)
1979/80				
11/8/79	1(L1)	A	Sheffield Wednesday	1–1 D
14/8/79	1(L2)	H	Sheffield Wednesday	1–2 L
				(Lost 3–1 on agg)

Date	Round	Venue	Opposition	Result
1978/79				
12/8/78	1(L1)	A	Peterborough United	0–1 L
15/8/78	1(L2)	H	Peterborough United	2–1 W
22/8/78	1R	A	Peterborough United	0–1 L
1977/78				
31/8/77	2	A	Southport	2–2 D
14/9/77	2R	H	Southport	1–0 W
25/10/77	3	H	Oldham Athletic	2–0 W
29/11/77	4	A	Arsenal	1–5 L
1976/77				
31/8/76	2	A	Leyton Orient	0–1 L
1975/76				
9/9/75	2	H	Preston North End	4–2 W
7/10/75	3	H	Sheffield United	2–0 W
11/11/75	4	A	Doncaster Rovers	1–2 L
1974/75				
2/9/74	2	H	Burnley	1–2 L
1973/74				
8/10/73	2	A	Leicester City	3–3 D
31/10/73	2R	H	Leicester City	3–2 W
6/11/73	3	H	Stockport County	4–1 W
27/11/73	4	H	Liverpool	0–0 D
4/12/73	4R	A	Liverpool	1–3 L
1972/73				
5/9/72	2	H	Fulham	2–1 W
3/10/72	3	H	Norwich City	1–2 L
1971/72				
7/9/71	2	A	Liverpool	0–3 L

Date	Round	Venue	Opposition	Result
1970/71				
9/9/70	2	A	West Ham United	0–1 L
1969/70				
3/9/69	2	H	Fulham	1–0 W
24/9/69	3	A	Derby County	1–3 L
1968/69				
14/8/68	1	A	Halifax Town	3–0 W
4/9/68	2	A	Brentford	0–3 L
1967/68				
12/9/67	2	A	QPR	1–2 L
1966/67				
24/8/66	1	A	Lincoln City	0–1 L
1965/66				
22/9/65	1	H	Derby County	2–2 D
27/9/65	1R	A	Derby County	3–4 L
1964/65				
22/9/64	1	H	Southend United	0–0 D
29/9/64	1R	A	Southend United	1–3 L
1963/64				
25/9/63	2	H	Exeter City	1–0 W
16/10/63	3	H	Manchester City	0–3 L
1962/63				
24/9/62	2	H	Middlesbrough	2–2 D
8/10/62	2R	A	Middlesbrough	1–1 D
10/10/62	2R2	H	Middlesbrough	3–0 W
17/10/62	3	H	Fulham	1–2 L

Date	Round	Venue	Opposition			Result
1961/62						
11/9/61	1	H	Bradford Park Avenue			4–2 W
3/10/61	2	A	Bury			4–3 W
15/11/61	3	A	Sunderland			1–2 L
1960/61						
10/10/60	1	H	Bolton Wanderers			0–0 D
19/10/60	1R	A	Bolton Wanderers			1–5 L

Totals:

P	W	D	L	F	A
Home					
55	24	14	17	75	72
Away					
61	9	10	42	61	133
Total					
116	33	24	59	136	205

PAWS FOR THOUGHT

The nickname 'the Tigers' originates from Hull City's choice of kit colours and has been associated with the club ever since the first black and amber shirt was worn by a City player in 1904. However, some people disagree and believe that shirts were changed to match the nickname – this seems unlikely as there would be no obvious reason to nickname a Humberside team the Tigers, particularly as there is minimal Asian wildlife in the area. Could the Tiger connection have come from the numerous frosty pitches the club have played on over the years (think about it!)? The less-popular nickname of 'the Boys from Boothferry' never caught on. What a shocker.

THE OVER-50s CLUB

There have been numerous players to score 50 goals or more for the Tigers – here is a list of the great and the good (their appearances and goals) who've reached the magical half-century wearing amber and black:

	League		FAC		LC		Other		Total	
	A	G	A	G	A	G	A	G	A	G
Chris Chilton										
	415	193	39	16	21	10	2	3	477	222
Ken Wagstaff										
	378	173	29	14	19	6	8	4	434	197
Sammy Stevens										
	150	84	11	9	0	0	30	23	191	116
Paddy Mills										
	269	101	22	9	0	0	0	0	291	110
John Smith										
	156	98	12	4	0	0	0	0	168	102
Keith Edwards										
	187	86	13	8	13	2	7	1	220	97
Ken Houghton										
	264	79	23	9	12	2	5	1	304	91
Bill Bradbury										
	178	82	12	7	0	0	0	0	190	89
Dean Windass										
	236	77	7	2	13	5	15	5	271	89
Doug Clark										
	368	79	31	6	12	2	0	0	411	87
Arthur Temple										
	173	77	11	4	0	0	0	0	184	81

League		FAC		LC		Other		Total	
A	G	A	G	A	G	A	G	A	G
Ian Butler									
305	68	22	4	9	0	3	0	339	72
John McSeveney									
161	60	12	8	10	2	0	0	183	70
Billy Whitehurst									
229	52	14	5	12	6	16	6	271	69
Stuart Elliott									
193	65	8	1	9	1	1	1	211	68
Andy Flounders									
159	54	13	4	8	3	11	2	191	63
Syd Gerrie									
146	59	6	3	0	0	0	0	152	62
Raich Carter									
136	57	14	5	0	0	0	0	150	62
Cliff Hubbard									
183	56	12	5	0	0	8	1	203	62
Ray Henderson									
229	54	33	6	12	1	0	0	274	61
Bill McNaughton									
85	57	7	2	0	0	0	0	92	59
Garreth Roberts									
414	47	28	5	24	2	21	5	487	59
George Martin									
204	55	14	3	0	0	0	0	218	58
Andy Payton									
143	55	8	0	11	2	3	0	162	57
Stanley Smith									
213	46	18	6	0	0	34	4	265	56

	League		FAC		LC		Other		Total	
	A	G	A	G	A	G	A	G	A	G
Viggo Jensen										
	308	51	27	3	0	0	0	0	325	54
Brian Marwood										
	158	51	16	1	5	0	12	1	191	53
Norman Moore										
	81	46	11	7	0	0	0	0	92	53
Alf Ackerman										
	92	49	11	2	0	0	0	0	103	51
Ken Harrison										
	238	47	25	4	0	0	0	0	263	51
Les Mutrie										
	115	49	8	1	6	0	3	0	132	50
Douglas Duncan										
	111	47	11	3	0	0	0	0	122	50
Russell Wainscoat										
	79	42	6	8	0	0	0	0	85	50

TAMPA PROOF

City and Tampa Bay Rowdies agreed to play perhaps the oddest two-legged tie in history back in 1984. After beating Tampa 3–0 at Boothferry Park in March, City flew out for a close-season mini-tour of the USA. Garreth Roberts scored the only goal in a 1–0 victory over Fort Lauderdale before the Tigers lost 1–0 to Tampa. However, they still won the Anglo-American Cup over Tampa, 3–1 on aggregate.

WATNEY CUP

City took part in The Watney Mann Invitation Cup – better known as the Watney Cup – on two occasions. Though it was a short-lived pre-season tournament, there were a number of firsts that make it stand-out somewhat from the numerous other meaningless competitions that hold little or no interest with the paying public.

The Watney Cup was held in the early 1970s and was contested by the teams that had scored the most goals in each of the four divisions of England and not been promoted or admitted to one of the European competitions. Two teams from each division took part, making eight participants in total. The competition was a straight knockout format, each match was a one-off with no replays. Unlike most other competitions, the final took place at the home ground of one of the finalists, rather than a neutral venue. It was one of the first competitions to be sponsored in English football (Watney were a major brewery at the time) and several Watney Cup matches were also televised live – a very rare occurrence in the '70s.

Running from 1970 to 1973, City's first match was against Peterborough United in 1970 and a crowd of nearly 10,000 saw the Tigers triumph 4–0 at London Road thanks to two goals each from Chris Chilton and Ken Wagstaff. That victory set up a clash with Manchester United and a bumper crowd of more than 34,000 packed into Boothferry Park to watch City take on perhaps the most famous club in the world. It also proved to be an historic occasion, with City and United inseperable on the day, drawing 1–1 after extra time. That led to the very first penalty shoot-out on English soil with George Best the first player to take and score a spot-kick in the shoot-out. Although Denis Law was also the first to miss, United eventually won 4–3 and progressed to the final where they lost 4–1 to Derby County.

City's next foray into the Watney Cup – the final year of the competition – was prior to the 1973/74 campaign. After they breezed past Mansfield Town with a 3–0 win at Field Mill, the Tigers edged out Bristol Rovers 1–0 at Eastville to earn a place in the final against Stoke City. Almost 20,000 crammed into the Victoria Ground but the hosts were too strong on their own patch and took the trophy with a 2–0 victory. All in all, the Watney Cup had proved both innovative and interesting for supporters and more than 81,000 fans watched the Tigers' five games in the tournament – an impressive average of 16,000 for each game.

NICK OF TIME …

The fastest goal on record for the Tigers is Nick Barmby's strike against Walsall in November 2004. Timed at just 8 seconds, City went on to win 3–1 while Barmby went on to write his name in the record books – and this one!

TIGER FEAT

No City fan will be particularly surprised to learn that the club's record victory came on the back of two awful defeats. After ending 1938 with two thrashings, to New Brighton (6–1) and Bradford City (6–2), the Tigers roared into 1939 by winning their first league game of the New Year 11–1 at home to Carlisle United. The 10-goal aggregate was nothing new, with City having beaten Halifax Town 10–0 nine years earlier, on Boxing Day 1930.

DARBY DAY!

Duane Darby will remember 26 November 1996 for the rest of his life after setting a club record during an FA Cup first round replay against Whitby Town. The first game ended 0–0 with both defences on top, but the replay suggests neither defence actually turned up in a remarkable game in which the teams shared 12 goals. Whitby came from behind to lead 4–3 with just seconds remaining – until Darby struck 49 seconds from time. The Tigers' superior fitness won the day in extra time with Darby completing a double hat-trick in an incredible 8–4 victory. Interestingly, despite a playing career which lasted more than 15 years and saw him play for six clubs, those goals were the only ones Darby ever managed in the FA Cup!

OLDEST/YOUNGEST

The oldest player to ever represent the Tigers is Eddie Burbanks, who was aged 40 years and 15 days when he played his final game for the club. The youngest player is Matthew Edeson, who was aged 16 years and 62 days when he made his City debut. Burbanks held the record of oldest player to score a goal for the club, too, until Dean Windass' effort against Portsmouth during the 2008/09 campaign was deemed his rather than an own goal. Deano was aged 39 years and 235 days at the time – a fitting epitaph for the big man and one that should stand for quite some time. Burbanks' goal, against Fulham in 1952, when he was aged 39 years and 193 days ensured he held the record for 57 years.

MOST CAPS

Theodore 'Tappa' Whitmore and Ian Goodison will always hold a fond place in the hearts of City fans. The 'Reggae Boyz' were close friends and Jamaican internationals when they joined City in 1999. Both were integral members of Jamaica's team in the 1998 World Cup and Whitmore scored the two goals in Jamaica's defeat of Japan. In the same year, Whitmore was also instrumental in helping Jamaica win the Caribbean Football Championship and was crowned the Caribbean Footballer of the Year.

Whitmore played for the Montego Bay Boys Club before representing Violet Kickers and then Seba United in Jamaica's National Premier League. In 1999 he received a free transfer to the Tigers, then in Division Three, and both he and Goodison stayed with the club until 2002 when the cash-strapped Tigers couldn't agree new deals. Whitmore won a club record 28 caps for Jamaica while with City, and Goodison won 26. Their departures were a disappointment for their legions of admirers on Humberside.

TIGER ROAR

Despite opposition from the national media who deemed Hull City to be nothing more than small fry, when the mighty Hungarian champions Vasas toured the country, Boothferry Park won a visit from arguably one of the most talented sides in the world.

The reason was the Tigers' floodlights – few clubs had them back in the mid-1950s – and could accommodate a midweek friendly. Vasas' itinerary included Wolves, Arsenal and Manchester City but after the Hungarians won those fixtures comfortably, few could see anything but an embarrassingly one-sided game against Hull. Fortunately, Vasas cared little about the press and attracted a crowd of 13,889 for the prestigious game with the locals keen to see a different brand of football – Hungary had become the first European side to take England apart at Wembley two years earlier, winning 6–3. So on a Monday evening in October 1955, the teams met and the Tigers turned in a fantastic performance, winning 3–1 with a hat-trick from Bill Bradbury. Fleet Street's reaction? Shhhhh!

SARDINE, ANYONE?

Yes, they were packed in like fishes in a tin when Man United visited Boothferry Park on 26 February 1949. It was a general boom-time for football clubs but Hull had never seen anything like it as FA Cup fever gripped the town.

Having seen off Accrington, Reading, Grimsby Town and Stoke, the Tigers were just two games away from their first FA Cup final and an incredible 55,019 fans packed into the ground to see if Division Three (North) minnows City could edge past the mighty Reds. Sadly, it wasn't to be with United winning 1–0 on the day, but the attendance record was set and is unlikely to ever be broken.

The most apathy shown by Tigers fans was for the games with Bradford City and Barnsley in 1916 and 1940 respectively, when estimated crowds of just 500 could be bothered turning up.

TRANSFERS FEES

The highest transfer fee forked out by the Tigers for a player was the £5m paid to Fulham for the services of Jimmy Bullard in January 2009. Going into the 2009/10 campaign, the highest fee received for a Hull City player is £4m for Michael Turner who joined Sunderland in 2009.

10 THINGS
YOU MAY NOT KNOW ABOUT
IAN ASHBEE

- Ash once spent time on loan to Icelandic side IR Knattspyrnudeild in 1996, playing eight games and scoring three goals during his spell.

- Signed by Jan Molby in 2002, Ash was sent off on his debut for the Tigers against Southend United – though his tough-tackling, industrious style soon won over the City fans and made him a natural candidate to become club captain.

- His spectacular goal against Yeovil Town in May 2004 won the Tigers promotion to League One with one game to spare.

- Ash has been diagnosed with an osteochondrial defect – a degenerative bone condition in his femur. He had to have surgery whereby 14 holes were drilled in the bone to stimulate regrowth, though he was warned by his doctor that the injury threatened not just his career, but his ability to even walk.

- Jan Molby, Peter Taylor, Phil Parkinson and Phil Brown have all chosen Ash to captain their teams and he has skippered the Tigers in all four divisions.

- His spectacular goal during a 4–1 win at Torquay was voted the club's Goal of the Season 2002/03.

- Birmingham-born Ash is, not surprisingly, a confirmed Birmingham City fan – there's no accounting for taste.

- In 2008 he won the Piers Morgan On Sport Sports Personality of the Year award.

- Ash spent more than two years with Derby County but only played one first-team game before moving on to Cambridge United where he spent six productive years.

- At the end of the 2008/09 campaign, Ash had played 481 times for his three clubs, but despite the fantastic service he's given over his 14-year career, he's never cost a penny in transfer fees to either Derby, Cambridge or City. He brought an end to his nine-year association with City when he surprisingly joined former boss Phil Brown at Preston in January 2011.

LAND OF GIANTS

City have been drawn against non-League opposition on 18 occasions in the FA Cup and played 23 games against clubs outside the top four divisions in total.

Morecambe are the only team the Tigers have actually been drawn more than once with, Blyth Spartans playing City on three occasions – though Blyth were only defeated after a second replay between the clubs. Out of 23 ties, only twice have City been subject to the feared 'giant-killing act' – in 2000 Kettering left Boothferry Park with a 1–0 win and, three years earlier, Hednesford also won 2–0 on Humberside. In alphabetical order, the full list is:

Bath City 3–0 W
Blyth Spartans 1–1 D, 2–2 D, 2–1 W
Crook Town 5–4 W
Gateshead 4–0 W
Hayes 2–2 D, 3–2 W
Hednesford Town 0–2 L
Kettering Town 0–0 D, 0–1 L
Kidderminster Harriers 4–1 W
Morecambe 1–0 W, 3–2 W
Northwich Victoria 5–2 W
Penrith 2–0 W
Rhyl Town 1–0 W
Salisbury Town 2–0 W
Stafford Rangers 2–1 W
Stalybridge Celtic 8–2 W
Sutton United 3–0 W
Whitby Town 0–0 D, 8–4 W
Total FA Cup non-League record:

P	W	D	L	F	A
23	16	5	2	61	27

FESTIVE FIXTURES – CHRISTMAS DAY

Christmas Day fixtures were commonplace in the football calendar until the mid-1950s – imagine what the legion of foreign players who moan for a complete winter break would make of that! While supporters would miss their football feast on Boxing Day, it's fair to say that most understand that Christmas Day is for families and not football, and that was the general consensus back in 1957 when the Tigers played their last 25 December fixture. As so often, it was a League double-header against the same team, with the return match on Boxing Day and in '57, City took on Gateshead at Boothferry Park, drawing 1–1 and losing 3–1 24 hours later. The first Christmas Day game in the League was in 1905, when City travelled to Port Vale and found their opponents to be in festive mood as they beat Vale 3–1. The two biggest Christmas victories were 5–1 wins over Wolves (1914) and Preston North End (1928), while a 6–2 tonking from Newcastle United at St James' Park in 1934 will remain the Tigers' worst defeat on that day. For the record, City's most common opponents at Christmas have been Darlington, with three matches against the Quakers in total.

The complete record is:

P	W	D	L
32	14	9	9

FESTIVE FIXTURES – BOXING DAY

Going into the 2012/13 campaign, the Tigers had played 78 matches on Boxing Day. One of the first games most supporters look for, a match on 26 December is usually a chance to stretch the legs and get a breath of fresh air after the indulgences of the previous day and, on average, the Tigers have fared reasonably well over the years on this date – though Phil Brown will probably leave the country on Boxing Day 2010! City won their first Boxing Day game at the first attempt, beating Burton United 3–0 away, but their first Premier League Boxing Day fixture was a disaster and after falling 4–0 to Manchester City, Tigers' boss Brown performed his infamous on-pitch half-time tirade at his players whom he seated in front of the 3,000 travelling fans. The second-half was better, but the Tigers still lost 5–1. A better memory is the 1930 26 December victory over Halifax Town – a 10–0 mauling watched by just over 4,000 fans. The two worst Boxing Day losses were in 1911 against Birmingham City and in 2008 against Manchester City, both by a score of 5–1. For the record, the Tigers have faced Hartlepool United more than any other on this date, with four meetings against the Monkey Hangers.

The complete record is:

P	W	D	L
78	33	14	31

CURTAIN-RAISERS

There's no day quite like it – the sun is shining, the pitch looking fantastic and a packed, expectant crowd waiting for the players to run out of the tunnel. OK, maybe that's painting too perfect a picture, but that's how most of us imagine the first day of the season is going to be.

For Tigers fans, the opening day of the new campaign has seen more heartache than joy, though it doesn't average out too badly. In fact, if the Tigers play against a team beginning with 'B', chances are that it will be a decent year for the club, with record opening day victories of 4–1 coming against Barnsley (1905), Blackpool (1912) and Burnley (1983) all proving profitable. City also beat Darlington by the same score in 2003. There have been three awful starts to the season, however, with Derby County (1924), Colchester (1960) and Oxford United (1994) all issuing heavy defeats to City. The team the Tigers have opened their season against most often is Blackpool and the complete record, including the 2–1 2009/10 opening day defeat to Chelsea, is:

P	W	D	L
96	31	27	38

QUAKER GLOATS

In 1960, City and Darlington became well and truly sick of each other following an epic FA Cup second-round battle that saw the teams meet each other four times in the space of 19 days. The first game, in the north-east, ended 1–1 and the replay at Boothferry Park two days later (watched by more than 18,000 people) also ended 1–1. A week later the teams reconvened at Doncaster's Bell Vue Ground but again couldn't be separated after a gruelling 0–0 draw. The fourth and decisive tie was held at Middlesbrough's Ayresome Park and this time the Tigers triumphed 3–0 in front of a crowd of almost 20,000. Of course, after all that effort, City ducked out in the next round, to Bolton Wanderers, the team who'd also eliminated them from the League Cup earlier in the season.

FAMILY THREE

Between 1905 and 1912 the Browell brothers represented City and on occasion, all three of the Northumberland-born siblings played in the same team.

George Browell, a stockily-built right wing-half, played 194 times for the Tigers between 1905 and 1911, while his younger brother Anthony ('Andy') Browell, a central defender, played for Hull between 1907 and 1912. The youngest of the trio, Thomas 'Boy' Browell, was undoubtedly the most talented. Eight years younger than eldest brother George, Tommy's path to City was eased by the reputation and popularity of his brothers though he was still only a teenager with Tyneside amateurs Newburn Grange.

So keen were two City directors to capture the talented forward that they even rowed a boat across to the colliery village where Tommy lived in order to sign him on. They succeeded and he joined the club in 1910 and went on to enjoy an explosive season on Humberside, scoring 32 goals in 48 appearances. In one game, against Stockport County, he scored a hat-trick and a journalist claimed that 'ten men and a boy beat Stockport' and from there on, Tommy was nicknamed 'Boy'. Word spread quickly of the prolific youngster who had made his debut for City aged 17 and after just over a year in league football, Everton paid the princely sum of £2 to take him to Merseyside and he later became a huge star at Manchester City, scoring 139 goals in 247 games.

FINDERS KEEPERS

Some days you just know things aren't going to go your way and on 31 January 1931, the City fans who travelled to Sincil Bank to watch the Tigers take on Lincoln City must have wondered whether they'd collectively run over a black cat on the way.

When goalkeeper Geordie Maddison was forced off injured, fiery left-back Ginger Bell went in goal instead. Of course, with no substitutes allowed, City were also now down to 10 men, too – but worse was around the corner. Bell, as ever, threw himself fully into his new role and was knocked unconscious shortly after! Arthur Childs deputised, but the sturdy centre-half could not prevent the inevitable as Lincoln City easily ran out 3–0 winners.

CITY v. THE REST OF THE WORLD

OK, maybe it's not quite the rest of the world, but here is a complete record of the Tigers' record against every other club in the land – and parts of Europe!! Easily the team City love to play against is the very first entry in the list below – Accrington Stanley (who are they!?). With a fantastic 18 wins from 25 games played against the Lancastrians, Accrington are the one team Tigers' fans can justifiably sing 'can we play you every week?' to. Barnsley are the team City have played more than any other, with 106 meetings recording between the two sides, and Lincoln City are not far behind with 103 meetings. The Tigers have pretty rotten records against Chelsea, Arsenal and Liverpool but then, doesn't everyone? The list, correct as of June 2009 is:

Opponents	Pld	W	D	L	Lg	FAC	LC	Oth
Accrington Stanley	25	18	5	2	24	1	0	0
Aldershot	4	2	1	1	4	0	0	0
Arsenal	7	1	1	5	2	2	3	0
Aston Villa	23	5	6	12	16	6	0	1
Bari	1	0	1	0	0	0	0	1
Barnet	12	2	5	5	12	0	0	0
Barnsley	106	41	21	44	92	2	0	12
Barrow	22	14	4	4	22	0	0	0
Bath City	1	1	0	0	0	1	0	0
Birmingham City	59	15	15	29	52	1	0	6
Blackburn Rovers	52	12	14	26	44	6	2	0
Blackpool	98	40	27	31	92	4	1	1
Blyth Spartans	3	1	2	0	0	3	0	0
Bolton Wanderers	45	9	15	21	36	5	4	0
Boston United	4	4	0	0	4	0	0	0
Bournemouth	41	18	11	12	40	0	0	1
Bradford City	92	37	18	37	70	2	0	20
Bradford P A	53	18	9	26	34	3	1	15

Opponents	Pld	W	D	L	Lg	FAC	LC	Oth
Brentford	54	26	11	17	48	5	1	0
Brighton & HA	42	12	10	20	40	2	0	0
Bristol City	73	23	19	31	70	2	0	1
Bristol Rovers	47	18	11	18	42	4	0	1
Burnley	50	18	11	21	48	1	1	0
Burton United	4	3	1	0	4	0	0	0
Bury	66	25	11	30	62	2	1	1
Cambridge United	16	10	2	4	16	0	0	0
Cardiff City	53	19	18	16	52	1	0	0
Carlisle United	78	32	22	24	70	5	2	1
Charlton Athletic	35	9	9	17	32	2	0	1
Chelsea	36	4	8	24	26	9	1	0
Cheltenham Town	10	4	2	4	8	2	0	0
Chester City	48	19	14	15	42	3	0	3
Chesterfield	40	22	10	8	34	0	0	6
Clapton Orient	40	20	11	9	40	0	0	0
Colchester United	31	11	9	11	30	1	0	0
Coventry City	43	18	8	17	34	2	3	4
Crewe Alexandra	40	23	7	10	34	4	1	1
Crook Town	1	1	0	0	0	1	0	0
Crystal Palace	42	18	13	11	38	2	2	0
Darlington	60	30	14	16	48	7	0	5
Denaby United	1	1	0	0	0	1	0	0
Derby County	50	17	16	17	44	0	4	2
Doncaster Rovers	48	20	9	19	40	1	1	6
Everton	12	5	3	4	6	6	0	0
Exeter City	34	21	6	7	32	1	1	0
Fiorentina	1	0	0	1	0	0	0	1
Fulham	83	29	26	28	76	5	2	0
Gainsborough T	16	9	3	4	14	0	0	2
Gateshead	27	10	4	13	22	3	0	2
Gillingham	14	4	4	6	13	0	0	0
Glossop	20	11	3	6	20	0	0	0
Grimethorpe United	1	1	0	0	0	1	0	0
Grimsby Town	77	33	19	25	46	1	4	26
Halifax Town	53	30	9	14	42	1	3	7

Opponents	Pld	W	D	L	Lg	FAC	LC	Oth
Hartlepool United	58	28	14	16	48	1	1	8
Hayes	2	1	1	0	0	2	0	0
Hednesford Town	1	0	0	1	0	1	0	0
Hereford United	8	3	3	2	8	0	0	0
Huddersfield Town	60	20	11	29	46	1	0	13
Ipswich Town	24	8	8	8	24	0	0	0
Kettering Town	2	0	1	1	0	2	0	0
Kidderminster	9	4	3	2	8	1	0	0
Lazio	1	1	0	0	0	0	0	1
Leeds City	32	13	10	9	22	2	0	8
Leeds United	47	13	9	25	38	0	0	9
Leicester City	78	31	22	25	62	4	3	9
Leigh RMI	1	1	0	0	0	0	0	1
Leyton Orient	51	16	20	15	46	2	1	2
Lincoln City	103	43	23	37	67	3	9	24
Liverpool	12	0	2	10	6	1	5	0
Luton Town	39	15	8	16	38	1	0	0
Macclesfield Town	18	5	8	5	12	4	2	0
Manchester City	19	5	5	9	12	4	1	2
Manchester United	21	5	3	13	16	2	2	1
Mansfield Town	51	19	14	18	46	1	0	4
Middlesbrough	52	14	16	22	36	7	3	6
Millwall	52	19	16	17	52	0	0	0
Milton Keynes Dons	2	1	1	0	2	0	0	0
Morecambe	2	2	0	0	0	2	0	0
Nelson	4	3	1	0	4	0	0	0
New Brighton	21	11	7	3	18	3	0	0
Newcastle United	23	5	4	14	8	7	1	7
Newport County	12	7	2	3	12	0	0	0
Northampton Town	17	7	3	7	16	1	0	0
Northwich Victoria	1	1	0	0	0	1	0	0
Norwich City	31	12	7	12	28	1	2	0
Nottingham Forest	62	23	7	32	52	2	0	8
Notts County	73	23	17	33	58	1	4	10
Oldham Athletic	77	30	21	26	70	5	1	1
Oxford United	42	12	14	16	42	0	0	0

Opponents	Pld	W	D	L	Lg	FAC	LC	Oth
Penrith	1	1	0	0	0	1	0	0
Peterborough Utd	34	9	8	17	30	0	3	1
Plymouth Argyle	74	32	19	23	68	6	0	0
Port Vale	68	29	15	24	62	4	0	2
Portsmouth	46	11	17	18	42	3	0	1
Preston North End	54	18	12	24	48	2	1	3
QPR	41	13	13	15	36	0	5	0
Reading	43	12	14	17	40	3	0	0
Rhyl	1	1	0	0	0	1	0	0
Rochdale	48	21	11	16	44	3	0	1
Rotherham County	16	7	5	4	8	0	0	8
Rotherham United	70	24	18	28	58	4	4	4
Runcorn	1	1	0	0	0	1	0	0
Rushden & D	4	1	2	1	4	0	0	0
Salisbury Town	1	1	0	0	0	1	0	0
Scarborough	13	5	2	6	6	0	4	3
Scunthorpe United	35	14	8	13	32	1	0	2
Sheffield United	65	16	20	29	44	2	3	16
Sheffield Wednesday	55	14	18	23	42	1	2	10
Shrewsbury Town	42	18	13	11	40	1	1	0
South Shields	18	7	3	8	18	0	0	0
Southampton	52	14	20	18	46	3	2	1
Southend United	36	13	13	10	34	0	2	0
Southport	30	19	5	6	23	5	2	0
Stafford Rangers	1	1	0	0	0	1	0	0
Stalybridge Celtic	1	1	0	0	0	1	0	0
Stockport County	78	28	27	23	70	5	3	0
Stockton	2	0	1	1	0	2	0	0
Stoke City	55	16	16	23	50	4	0	1
Sunderland	30	10	5	15	26	3	1	0
Sutton Town	1	1	0	0	0	1	0	0
Swansea City	63	22	14	27	62	1	0	0
Swindon Town	40	8	15	17	40	0	0	0
Torquay United	28	12	8	8	28	0	0	0
Tottenham Hotspur	20	5	7	8	14	6	0	0
Tranmere Rovers	35	21	4	10	32	1	1	1

Opponents	Pld	W	D	L	Lg	FAC	LC	Oth
Verona	1	1	0	0	0	0	0	1
Walsall	26	13	7	6	26	0	0	0
Watford	36	13	13	10	30	3	1	2
West Brom	46	16	12	18	42	3	0	1
West Ham United	35	9	13	13	32	2	1	0
Whitby Town	2	1	1	0	0	2	0	0
Wigan Athletic	17	5	6	6	14	1	2	0
Wimbledon	8	3	3	2	8	0	0	0
Wolves	58	25	11	22	52	4	2	0
Woolwich Arsenal	4	1	2	1	2	2	0	0
Workington	9	4	1	4	8	1	0	0
Wrexham	44	16	8	20	38	3	2	1
Wycombe Wanderers	4	2	2	0	4	0	0	0
Yeovil Town	2	1	1	0	2	0	0	0
York City	67	27	18	22	50	2	0	15

STAN THE MAN

One of the most famous players to don a Hull City shirt was the great Stan Mortensen. The hugely popular forward had made his name before the Second World War with Blackpool. After becoming the first man to score a hat-trick in an FA Cup final in 1953 – better known as 'The Matthews Final' – aged 34, in November 1955 he left the Seasiders and joined the Tigers for a fee of £2,000. Mortensen, with 25 England caps between 1947 and 1953, was a huge name at the time and his home debut against West Ham attracted a crowd of 24,050 – easily the best Boothferry Park crowd of the season. The great man didn't disappoint either, scoring in a 3–1 victory – one of 18 goals in 42 appearances for the club before he joined Southport in 1957.

MINE'S A TREBLE

Club legend and record goal-scorer Chris Chilton is arguably the greatest predator the Tigers have ever had and he was one of the most feared – and gifted – lower league strikers in the country.

He played for City between 1959 and 1971 and scored a club record 11 hat-tricks during his time at Boothferry Park. His first treble came in 1960 when, aged 17, he scored all City's goals in a 3–1 win over QPR and scored another just under a year later in a 4–1 win over Millwall. Two months later his triple tally helped dispatch Bristol City 4–0 and in October 1963, he went one better, scoring all four goals in a 4–2 win over Wrexham. Later in the 1963/64 campaign he scored another hat-trick – this time against Notts County – and the following season he bagged four against Barnsley in a 7–0 victory and another three 20 days later in a 3–1 victory at Brentford.

Hat-trick number 8 came in October 1965 against Oldham Athletic and he bagged his ninth treble against Exeter City the following April. Hat-trick number 10 came in December 1966 against Crystal Palace and it took another five years before he managed his eleventh and final treble in an amazing career, when he again collected the match-ball for his three goals during a 4–0 win over Sunderland. He joined Coventry City seven months later for £92,000 but the Hull public showed their appreciation to this most amazing striker by turning out in their thousands for his testimonial against Leeds United in which, inevitably, he scored a hat-trick in a 7–6 win, watched by more than 28,000 fans at Boothferry Park.

10 THINGS YOU MAY (OR MAY NOT KNOW) ABOUT STEVE BRUCE

- His middle name is Roger.

- He was born in Corbridge, Northumberland.

- Bruce had numerous trials with many top clubs before Gillingham gave him a chance to build a career.

- He is a Newcastle United fan – his club since his schooldays.

- Steve was a ball boy at the 1974 League Cup final between Wolves and Man City.

- Had he not made the grade as a footballer, Steve would probably now be a plumber.

- Bruce started life at Gillingham as a midfielder – his friend Peter Beardsley was turned down by the Gills around the same time.

- His first season with Gillingham saw him finish top scorer for the reserves with 18 goals!

- Bruce began life as a Norwich player by scoring an own goal in the first minute of his debut!

- Apart from his autobiography, Steve has written three published novels about a fictional footballer called Steve Barnes.

THE SHORTEST SEASON

City spent the entire 1939/40 Division Three (North) season unbeaten and didn't lose a League game until Southport beat the Tigers 3–1 at Haig Avenue in September 1946. Alas, this wasn't a hitherto little-known golden era of the club's history, but was due to the outbreak of the Second World War. Just two games into the 1939/40 season and having drawn their League games against Lincoln City and Southport, football was suspended in England. It would be seven years before City took part in Division Three (North) again and they opened their campaign, just as they'd started their last, with two draws, against Lincoln City and Crewe Alexandra.

CLOSE GAME ...

The people of Hull and the players of Hull City are still frowned upon in Germany after the Tigers travelled to Europe on a brief tour. City beat a hapless Solingen 16–0 on 14 May 1910 with George Temple bagging a double hat-trick and Joe Smith scoring three during a game the locals never really came to terms with. Two days later, City thrashed Sparta Rotterdam 4–1 to complete a successful European PR exercise!

STREAKER ALERT!

City's record streaks are as follows:

Successive wins: 10 – 1/5/1948 – 8/9/48

Successive losses: 8 – 7/4/1934 – 8/9/34

Longest unbeaten run: 18 – 23/10/1948 – 12/2/1949

Longest run of games without winning: 16 – 15/2/1936 – 2/5/1936

To put some meat on the bones of the above stats, the most enjoyable entry is without doubt the 10 consecutive League wins the Tigers enjoyed in 1948. Overlapping the end of 1947/48 season and the start of one of the best seasons the club has ever enjoyed, the 1948/49 campaign, all the victories were in Division Three (North). City ended 1947/48 with a 3–1 home win over Carlisle United and began the new season with a 2–1 victory at Tranmere Rovers. The August Bank Holiday weekend saw City crush Oldham Athletic 6–0 and then hammer Mansfield Town 4–0 at home before travelling north to beat Barrow 2–1. Accrington Stanley and Wrexham were beaten 3–0 and 3–1 respectively and then Halifax Town were humbled 4–2 at The Shay. Bradford City and Accrington Stanley (again) became victims number 9 and 10 before Doncaster Rovers ended the winning streak with a 0–0 draw at Belle Vue. City went on to become champions that season, winning the League in a canter and finishing 15 points ahead of third-placed Doncaster. That season also saw an unbeaten run of 18 games that included 12 wins and six draws, though six of those games formed part of an epic FA Cup run and was ended by a 4–2 defeat away to Bradford City – the

Tigers only loss on the road all season and to a team that would finish bottom of the table!

The Tigers' record losing run is eight, stretching from April 1934 to September the same year, though there were times during the second half of the 2008/09 Premier League campaign that threatened to update or at least equal that run. It began with a 1–0 home defeat to Grimsby Town and then Bradford Park Avenue beat City 3–1. The Tigers then completed a miserable season by losing 1–0 at home to Preston North End, 7–0 at Oldham Athletic and 1–0 at home to Burnley. Just like winning, losing becomes a hard habit to break and despite bagging four goals at Home Park against Plymouth Argyle, City conceded half-a-dozen in an amazing 6–4 reverse. A 2–1 defeat at Blackpool and a 1–0 loss at home to Bury made it eight before a 1–1 draw at home to Plymouth finally stopped the rot.

Season 1935/36 would end in relegation from Division Two for City and it would also see a dismal run of 16 games without a victory. After a fine 1–0 away win at Plymouth, the Tigers couldn't buy a win and suffered a number of woeful Saturday afternoons, particularly away to Doncaster Rovers and Swansea Town who each dished out 6–1 thrashings. Ironically, City finished the season on something of a high, holding third-placed Sheffield United and champions Manchester United to draws at Anlaby Road. Those two results, coupled with a fantastic start to the 1936/37 campaign, formed part of an unbeaten run of 11 games – typical City! From one extreme to the other!

THE TIGERS – A POTTED HISTORY...

1904 – Hull City Football Club is founded and the fledgling club begin life playing friendly games at The Boulevard, home of Hull Rugby League, Dairycoates and the Anlaby Road Cricket Ground.

1904 – City make a permanent home of Anlaby Road and the club will remain there until 1941.

1906 – After winning a place in the Football League, the Tigers finish their first season in Division Two in a highly-creditable fifth place.

1910 – Thanks to the amber and black striped shirts, City are nicknamed 'the Tigers' and the club misses out on promotion to the top-flight by 0.29 of a goal to Oldham Athletic – the narrowest margin in the history of English football.

1915 – After a 4–1 win over Grimsby Town, the First World War sees football in England suspended with the Tigers forced to play matches in a 14-strong Midlands league.

1919 – City return to Division Two football with a 4–1 defeat at Birmingham City.

1930 – After a decade of mid-table mediocrity, the Tigers embark on a record-breaking FA Cup run that sees them knock out First Division Newcastle United and Manchester City before losing in the semi-final to Arsenal. The club's cup exploits take their toll on a wafer thin squad and City are relegated to Division Three (North), for the first time, on the goal average rule.

1933 – City roar back, winning Division Three (North) after scoring 100 goals and amassing 59 points.

1936 – Just five wins from 42 and 111 goals conceded sees the Tigers relegated again.

1939 – Football is again suspended in England and it will be seven years before the Tigers return to league action.

1941 – Dire finances mean that, effectively, Hull City FC cease to exist while the Second World War continues – many wonder whether Hull will ever see the return of its team.

1944 – City return to War League action for one season but then go back into hibernation for 12 months.

1946 – With the war over, City resume life in Division Three (North) with a 0–0 draw against Lincoln City at their new, purpose built stadium, Boothferry Park. The people of Hull flock to the new ground to see the Tigers and a crowd of 25,586 watch the match.

1948 – Manager Raich Carter guides City to the Division Three (North) title and the Tigers set a divsional attendance record of 49,655 for the Christmas Day home clash with Rotherham United.

1949 – Another club record is posted after more than 55,000 people pack into Boothferry Park to see the Tigers take on Manchester United in the FA Cup sixth round.

1956 – City are relegated to Division Three (North).

1959 – City return to Division Two, but their stay in the second tier is brief and they are relegated after just one season.

1966 – The Tigers win the 1965/66 Division Three (North) title after a record-breaking campaign that sees the club score 109 goals and gather 69 points and reach the quarter-final of the FA Cup, losing to Chelsea after a replay.

1971 – Player-manager Tery Neill guides City to their best post-war finish of fifth place in Division Two, and the Tigers again reach the last eight of the FA Cup, losing out 3–2 to Stoke City despite leading 2–0!

1978 – After a relatively uneventful decade, City return to Division Three after 12 years in the second tier.

1981 – The Tigers drop into the Fourth Division for the first time.

1982 – The club's persistent financial problems finally result in the Tigers being placed into receivership.

1983 – With new chairman Don Robinson in control, City win promotion to Division Three.

1984 – Needing to win by three goals to secure a second successive promotion, City beat Burnley 2–0 at Turf Moor and agonisingly miss out to Sheffield United who, despite having the same goal difference, had scored more goals in total.

1985 – City have to wait just 12 months before winning a place in Division Two.

1991 – After numerous managerial upheavals, the Tigers are again relegated to Division Three.

1996 – City slump into the nation's lowest tier for only the second time in 90 years.

1997 – After a disappointing campaign, the Tigers post a record-low finish of 16th in the fourth division.

1998 – The Tigers surpass their previous worst by finishing in 22nd in the lowest league in English football – just two places lower and City would have been playing in the Conference!

2000 – Boothferry Park gates locked and the club effectively kicked out of their own ground – eventually players and officials are allowed to return though the club's financial position remains precarious.

2001 – A new owner, Adam Pearson, takes control of the club, heralding a bright new era on Humberside.

2002 – City move to their new home, the £43.5m KC Stadium, in December, located within a stone's throw of their original home at Anlaby Road. The first official League game sees City beat Hartlepool 2–0 on Boxing Day in front of 22,319 fans.

2004 – On the crest of a wave, the Tigers finally emerge from their eight-year stay in the basement division by finishing runners-up in Division Three.

2005 – A second successive promotion for the Tigers who continue their dramatic resurgence up the leagues.

2006 – City struggle in the Championship, finishing in 18th place.

2007 – The Tigers narrowly avoid relegation under new manager Phil Brown.

2008 – One of Hull City's favourite sons, Dean Windass, volleys home a dramatic play-off final winner against

Bristol City to send the Tigers into the top flight for the first time in the club's history.

2009 – City survive relegation on the final day of their inaugural Premier League season. Despite losing to Manchester United and only winning once in their final 23 matches, the Tigers fans celebrate as though the team had won the FA Cup!

2010 – In March, manager Phil Brown is put on gardening leave. In May, a 2–2 draw at Wigan confirms the Tigers' relegation from the Premier League.

2011 – Bristol City end the Tigers' 17-match unbeaten run – a new club record.

2012 – Nick Barmby guides City to an eighth-place finish in the Championship but his tenure is ended after his criticism of the club's owners lands him in hot water. Steve Bruce is subsequently named manager.

ANGLO-SCOTTISH CUP

The Tigers have taken part in the Anglo-Scottish Cup on four occasions, without ever winning the trophy – or taking on Scottish opponents. The competition has never garnered more than a passing interest among the City fans, a fact reflected in the disappointing crowds that dogged the tournament during its existence. The first match the Tigers took part in was back in August 1975 when Leicester City visited Boothferry Park, leaving with a 1–1 draw. Just 3,524 turned out for the game and even fewer attended the second group game, also at home, against West Bromwich Albion – 3,054 saw the Baggies win 2–1 and a 2–1 defeat at Mansfield Town completed a miserable pre-season warm-up for City. The following season saw a little more interest in the competition, but not much more in terms of success. A 2–0 defeat at Middlesbrough was watched by almost 7,000 at Ayresome Park and then it was back to Boothferry where City entertained the losing League Cup finalists, Newcastle United. A crowd of 4,715 saw the Tigers grind out a respectable 0–0 draw and despite beating old adversaries Sheffield United 1–0 at home in the final group game, City hadn't done enough to progress into the final stages.

The tournament took on the tag of an annual contest at the start of the 1977/78 campaign, but the people of Humberside had already had their fill of a competition in which they had, bizarrely, still not taken on a side from north of the border. A 1–0 defeat at Notts County was followed by a 2–0 home reverse to Sheffield United and, with qualification impossible, just 1,618 people could bother watching City and Oldham Athletic draw 1–1 at Boothferry Park.

City sat out the next two seasons before returning for one last hurrah in 1980. More than 5,000 watched City beat Grimsby Town 1–0 at home but Sheffield United (again!) virtually ended hopes of finally making it through to the next phase with a 2–1 win at Bramall Lane. The Tigers' final match was at Saltergate where a 1–1 draw with eventual cup-winners Chesterfield proved to be the club's final appearance in the tournament. The complete record and details of each group are:

1975/76
NB: Bonus points (**B**) for scoring three goals

Group 2
Hull City 1–1 Leicester City
West Bromwich Albion 1–1 Mansfield Town
Hull City 1–2 West Bromwich Albion
Mansfield Town 2–0 Leicester City
Mansfield Town 2–1 Hull City
Leicester City 2–1 West Bromwich Albion

	Pld	W	D	L	F	A	B	Pts
1 Mansfield Town	3	2	1	0	5	2	0	5
2 West Brom	3	1	1	1	4	4	0	3
3 Leicester City	3	1	1	1	3	4	0	3
4 Hull City	3	0	1	2	3	5	0	1

1976/77

Group 4
Middlesbrough 2–0 Hull City
Sheffield United 0–1 Newcastle United
Hull City 0–0 Newcastle United
Sheffield United 0–1 Middlesbrough
Hull City 1–0 Sheffield United
Newcastle United 3–0 Middlesbrough

	Pld	W	D	L	F	A	Pts
1 Newcastle United	3	2	1	0	4	0	5
2 Middlesbrough	3	2	0	1	3	3	4
3 Hull City	3	1	1	1	1	2	3
4 Sheffield United	3	0	0	3	0	3	0

1977/78
NB: Bonus points (**B**) for scoring three goals

Group 4
Notts County 1–0 Hull City
Oldham Athletic 2–3 Sheffield United
Oldham Athletic 0–0 Notts County
Hull City 0–2 Sheffield United
Sheffield United 4–5 Notts County
Oldham Athletic 1–1 Hull City

	Pld	W	D	L	F	A	B	Pts
1 Notts County	3	2	1	0	6	4	1	6
2 Sheffield United	3	2	0	1	9	7	2	6
3 Oldham Athletic	3	0	2	1	3	4	0	2
4 Hull City	3	0	1	2	1	4	0	1

Play-off
Notts County 3–0 Sheffield United

1980/81
NB: Bonus points (**B**) for scoring three goals

Group 1
Hull City 1–0 Grimsby Town
Chesterfield 1–0 Sheffield United
Grimsby Town 3–3 Chesterfield
Sheffield United 2–1 Hull City
Chesterfield 1–1 Hull City
Sheffield United 0–1 Grimsby Town

	Pld	W	D	L	F	A	B	Pts
1 Chesterfield	3	1	2	0	5	4	1	5
2 Grimsby Town	3	1	1	1	4	4	1	4
3 Hull City	3	1	1	1	3	3	0	3
4 Sheffield United	3	1	0	2	2	3	0	2

Total Anglo-Scottish record:

Pld	W	D	L	F	A
12	2	4	6	8	14

CARETAKER MANAGERS

There have been several caretaker bosses of the Tigers over the years – here is a summary of the temporary bosses and their record while in the hot-seat.

Chris Chilton, December 1979

Club legend Chris Chilton took charge of three games in December '79 before being replaced by Mike Smith. He took command prior to the Tigers' Christmas programme, losing 1–0 at home to Blackburn before drawing 2–2 at Blackpool on Boxing Day. A 3–0 defeat at Oxford United was his final game in charge.

Bobby Brown/Chris Chilton, March 1982–August 1982

Chilton returned to the hot-seat in 1982, this time accompanied by Bobby Brown. Though the pair lost their first game 2–1 at Wigan Athletic, City won their next four games on the bounce to move up the table and away from any danger of relegation. Away defeats at Darlington and Colchester United followed but successive wins over Rochdale and Hereford United made it six wins from eight, leading to calls for the duo to be given the job on a permanent basis. Just two more defeats in their final 10 games in charge and an eighth-place finish in Division Four, many felt, was enough to suggest Brown and Chilton could take the Tigers to promotion the following season, but after three games of the Football League Trophy during the 1982/83 pre-season, the board turned instead to Colin Appleton.

Chris Chilton, May 1984

After Colin Appleton's shock resignation at the end of the 1983/84 campaign, it was Chris Chilton who again stepped into the breach. With the League programme over and just two Associate Member Cup games to be played before the summer break, Chilton took command of a 4–1 win over Tranmere Rovers and a 2–1 home defeat to Bournemouth before Brian Horton took the reins.

Tom Wilson/ Dennis Booth, April 1988–May 1988

Tom Wilson and Dennis Booth ushered out the 1987/88 campaign following Brian Horton's departure and did a decent job of their four matches in charge. Safe from relegation in mid-table, the duo's first game was a 4–0 home win over Huddersfield Town and they followed that result with a 1–1 draw at West Brom. More than 10,000 City fans watched the Tigers lose their final home game of the season 1–0 to Millwall and a 0–0 draw at Reading completed their reign before Eddie Gray took command.

Tom Wilson, October 1989–November 1989

Tom Wilson was back in temporary charge just six months later following Gray's sacking. He only held the hot-seat for a few days, guiding the Tigers to successive 0–0 draws with Blackburn Rovers and Watford prior to Stan Ternent taking over.

Tom Wilson, January 1991

Wilson's third spell as caretaker was less successful than his previous tenures. The Tigers were on their way to finishing bottom of Division Two and Wilson couldn't prevent a club in turmoil losing 5–2 at home to Notts County in the FA Cup and successive League defeats against Sheffield Wednesday and Swindon Town. Even the arrival of new boss Terry Dolan couldn't save the Tigers who slipped back into the third tier four months later.

Billy Russell, April 2000

Billy Russell began the first of three caretaker manager roles in the space of just two years in April 2000 following Warren Joyce's departure. Despite City winning three successive games, Joyce left Humberside and Russell began with a match at Northampton Town and, though the Tigers put up a decent display, the Cobblers won 1–0. Mid-table was not quite out of reach, but a 3–1 loss at home to Barnet compounded a miserable season in the bottom division. Russell ended his reign with a 1–0 win at Plymouth Argyle before Brian Little took command for the final game of the campaign.

Billy Russell, March 2002–April 2002

Russell resumed command for seven games in 2002. Brian Little had left the club following a 1–0 home loss to Macclesfield Town and the ever-dependable Russell was more than happy to take on team affairs. His first task was to pick up points at Swansea City, but the Tigers lost the game 1–0 – exactly the same result Russell had started his first spell in 2000 with. A 4–1 win over Mansfield Town was pleasing, but losing to rivals Scunthorpe United at home four days later was not. Just two goals and four more defeats in the next four games meant Russell had lost seven of his 11 matches in charge and he happily handed over control to new boss Jan Molby in early April.

Billy Russell, October 2002

After just seven months in charge, Molby was sacked following a 1–0 defeat to his former club, Kidderminster Harriers. Russell started his third spell in charge with a comprehensive 3–0 win over Rochdale, but new boss Peter Taylor was installed in time for the next game.

Phil Brown, December 2006

With Phil Parkinson enduring an awful season and the Tigers looking a good bet for relegation, Phil Brown stepped into the breach when Parkinson was fired after a dreadful run of results.

Brown had the experience of managing having been Derby County boss prior to his arrival at the KC Stadium but a 1–0 defeat at Plymouth hardly helped his cause. The City fans got behind Brown straight from the off and the biggest crowd of the season – 23,089 – turned up for his first home game in charge and were rewarded with a 4–1 win over Cardiff City. A 0–0 draw with Leeds United, a narrow defeat at Leicester City and a 2–0 home win over Burnley convinced the board that Brown deserved the post permanently, thus becoming the first caretaker to continue in the role and, as they say, the rest is history.

BRIGHT SPARK

David Brightwell played for the Tigers during the 2000/01 season, making 27 appearances and scoring one goal. Former Manchester City defender David, brother of Ian Brightwell, certainly came from good stock – he is the son of Olympic gold medallist Ann Packer and 400m runner Robbie Brightwell.

PHIL BROWN'S SCHOOL DAYS

Indoctrinated by his parents, Phil Brown was a boyhood Sunderland supporter but during his school days he was taught by 10,000m Olympic-bronze medal winning runner Brendan Foster – a die-hard Newcastle United fan!

BROWNY SAID IT…

'We had hoped to meet with Michael Owen before we went to Italy but when you're up against Manchester United, you know you're on the back-foot. To be in a two-horse race with Manchester United for an England international gives me great pride. He was ready to consider coming to Hull City but he has joined the champions of England. You can't argue with that but for me it was positive to see us in the running.'

The City boss, pleased to be up there with the best

'I'm disappointed but I was always nervous about the deal because of the way it was dragging along. But things happen for a reason and as far as Hull City are concerned, the only ones I'm interested in getting through the door are players who want to play for the club.'

Browny on Fraizer Campbell's move to Sunderland

'I took a phone call from Sir Alex and he was apologetic that the player had not come to us. He firmly believed this was the right club for Fraizer but he's obviously getting advice from somewhere else.'

**The Tigers' boss reveals
even Sir Alex couldn't
convince Campbell**

'We're disappointed but as resilient people we dust ourselves down and get on with the next one and hopefully that will whet the whistle. There's constant work going on behind the scenes. It's difficult getting the right players I must admit. But we're not panicking; fans need to know there's still a lot of work going on in the background.'

**The Tigers boss on the problem
of convincing big names to
move to the KC**

BY ROYAL APPOINTMENT?

City have had several players at the club over the years with distinguished surnames. There have been two Kings – David John (1957–63) and Marlon (2008–9), one Prince – Arthur (1928–29) and two Lords, Barry (1954–61) and Malcolm (1964–80).

SUM TOTAL

At the end of the 2008/09 campaign, statto.com compiled an all-time table of English league clubs taking into account every league result from each club's inception. The good news is the Tigers made the top 40 in 30th place, ahead of the likes of Middlesbrough, Tottenham and Leeds United. The top three are fairly predictable with Manchester United, Liverpool and Arsenal taking the first three berths.

City's total record to date is:

Pld	W	D	L	GD	Pts
4136	1549	1101	1486	+202	4691

The Tigers lie in 64th in the overall complete FA Cup record, trailing clubs such as Darwen and Aldershot! A good FA Cup run in 2012/13 could see them overhaul the likes of Fulham, Middlesbrough and Portsmouth, but until then, the overall record is as follows:

Pld	W	D	L	F	A	GD
266	99	72	95	391	374	+17

Finally, City's League Cup record is the worst of all the domestic competitions the club has taken part in over the years. Lying in 83rd position, City need to improve their League Cup stats dramatically if they are break into the top 79! Such luminaries as Bradford Park Avenue and Scarborough have better records than the Tigers, so a few good League Cup runs are needed sooner rather than later!

The overall record is:

Pld	W	D	L	F	A	GD
121	34	25	62	141	213	-71

BOAZ SAID IT ...

'I've certainly discovered a lot about myself. I missed ten games when the manager changed the team around, brought in Matt Duke and that wasn't a good feeling.'

'It's been a mental adjustment as much as anything. You're up against very good players in every game, which means there will be periods when the opposition are on top and you have to work incredibly hard just stay in the game.'

Boaz on life at the top

'Then there will be times when the goalkeeper is out of the game, but even then you have to be constantly alert because when the balls do come into the box, the delivery is so good. Picking and choosing when to intervene is key and again, experience is a factor.'

'Players will react differently to different situations but it has given us renewed impetus to put on a good performance in front of our home fans. It is up to the manager to manage his players how he feels best. It's up to the players to take that on board and produce a good performance. We are all disappointed; nobody goes on the pitch to do that purposefully. Obviously it is up to us to pick up the pieces.'

Boaz on THAT team talk at Manchester City

LET THERE BE LIGHT

The Tigers' first League match played under floodlights was on 8 January 1955 when 8,155 fans watched City and Doncaster Rovers play out a 1–1 draw at Boothferry Park.

CITY ON STAGE...

Tigers fan Alan Plater wrote a play on City that was first staged in 2004 called *Confessions of a City Supporter*. Featuring four generations of a family of Hull City supporters, each with a tale to tell, the play was originally written at the time the club celebrated its centenary. Plater has since updated his work to include the triumphant promotion to the Premier League.

In the 2009 version, Martin Barrass plays the youngest member of the family and his family's devotion to Hull City is more about duty and tradition than obsession.

Lifelong City fan Roy North, of 1970s Basil Brush fame, plays a succession of grandfathers, fathers and a rattle-waving youngster. The production was still doing good business at the Hull Truck Theatre in 2009.

SOMETHING IN RESERVE...

The Tigers' reserve team plays their home games at North Ferriby United's Church Road Ground, with a capacity of 2,700 and its location close to Hull (just 8 miles outside the city).

CAN WE PLAY YOU EVERY WEEK?

Of the 22 League meetings between the Tigers and Southport, City have won all 11 home games. It's the only 100 per cent record City have against anyone who they've met more than 10 times in total.

Total home record:
Pld 11   W 11   D 0   L 0   F 40   A 9

CAN WE PLAY YOU EVERY WEEK? – 2

Chesterfield have never won away to Hull City AFC – and as Rafa Benitez says, 'that's a fact!' City have won 13 and drawn four of the 17 games on Humberside and have never tasted defeat – a fantastic record. The Tigers' record at Saltergate isn't too bad either, having lost just five of the 17 visits to Derbyshire.

City's total record is:
Pld 34   W 20   D 9   L 5   F 62   A 25

CAN WE PLAY YOU EVERY WEEK? – 3

Accrington Stanley are, according to our records, the Tigers favourite opposition. In 24 meetings with the Lancastrians, City have won 17, drawn five and lost just twice in total scoring 51 times and conceding 23 – shame we don't play them more often!

DEVON HELP THEM!

Exeter City must shudder every time they travel to Humberside with an appalling record over the years. City have won 12 of the 16 games at home and the away record is pretty decent too, having won 7 and drawn 3 of the 16 fixtures at St James' Park.

The complete record is:

Home:	Pld 16	W 12	D 3	L 1	F 43	A 16
Away:	Pld 16	W 7	D 3	L 6	F 23	A 21
Total:	Pld 32	W 19	D 6	L 7	F 66	A 37

THE FULL MONTY

The Tigers do not enjoy travelling to Sheffield – full stop! There is no other city in England that Hull have quite as bad a League record as they do in the Steel City – even Manchester and London fare better, and that's saying something. Sheffield Wednesday is the worst with Bramall Lane only slightly better, though the records are almost identical – here's why:

at Hillsborough:	Pld 21	W 3	D 5	L 13	F 20	A 50
at Bramall Lane:	Pld 23	W 4	D 6	L 13	F 25	A 59
Sheffield record:	Pld 44	W 7	D 11	L 26	F 45	A 109

Add the fact that the Blades have only lost 5 times in 22 visits to Hull and you've got a bona fide bogey team – 8 wins in 44 tells its own story.

OTHER NOTABLE RECORDS...

City have lost just 4 of the 31 home fixtures they've played against Port Vale, while Wrexham have won just 4 of their 19 visits to City, though in the reverse fixture, the Tigers have won just 3 of their 19 trips to the Racecourse Ground.

Millwall at home usually yields points for the Tigers who have lost just 2 of the 26 League fixtures against the Lions, but again, the corresponding match in London has seen City win just three times in 26 visits.

Chelsea at Stamford Bridge is pretty dire with no victories at all, 3 draws and 12 losses in 15 matches and just 3 goals! Barnet have won 4 of their 6 visits to Humberside, losing only once to date and City have won just once away to Barnet – 2 wins in 12 ain't that impressive!

The Tigers have won 13 of their 23 visits to Darlington including the last three trips to the north-east.

BROWNY SAID IT ...

'You do desperately try to hang on to your better players. People have classed the price tag on Michael Turner as ridiculous at £10 million. I think he is worth that to us, it might not be worth that to somebody else, but he is to us. As far as we are concerned that is how big a player he is for us. Michael played 38 games for us last year and never missed a minute. He is being courted by bigger clubs because of the way he can defend.'

PB on Michael Turner

'We've tried to improve three things from last season. For a start, six clean sheets wasn't enough. Then, our goals from midfield wasn't enough. If you exclude Geovanni, because he's between a striker and a midfielder, one goal – possibly two if you count Bernard Mendy – wasn't enough. Dean Marney needs to improve to do that; George Boateng needs to improve that; we brought Hunty in to improve that; we bought Kamel Ghilas to do that and Seyi Olofinjana hopefully can do that from set pieces. After that we need a striker to round it all off and maybe get into double figures. If we can improve those three areas it bodes well for the season and it means we can finish higher than 17th – and that's all we're hoping for.'

Browny reveals his blueprint for the 2009/10 campaign

'The lad has decided to stay in Spain. We did everything we possibly could and I take my hat off to the chairman for the things he did in getting a world-class player to even talk to us. But that's dead now, it's on the wave behind and we'll try to get the next one. I'm very disappointed. There was a lot of effort and energy, not just from myself – for the last six weeks we were working hard at it.'

PB on Alvaro Negredo's decision to not become the Tigers' first acquisition from Real Madrid

MERSEY SIGHS!

Tranmere Rovers are another side who must turn green every time they approach Hull. The Wirral outfit has consistently been awful on their Tiger travels – their last visit ended in a 6–1 mauling.

City's record against Tranmere is:

Home:	P 16	W 12	D 1	L 3	F 36	A 11
Away:	P 16	W 6	D 3	L 7	F 27	A 29
Total:	P 32	W 18	D 4	L 10	F 63	A 30

10 THINGS YOU PROBABLY DIDN'T KNOW ABOUT SEYI OLOFINJANA

- His full name is Oluwaseyi George Olofinjana.

- 'Seyi' is a nickname meaning 'God made this'.

- He was born on 30 June 1980 in Lagos, Nigeria.

- City are his fourth English club having had spells with Arsenal, Wolverhampton Wanderers and Stoke City prior to his move to the Tigers.

- Aged 19, he made his debut for Nigeria during a 3–2 win over Malawi – he has since won 45 caps for the Super Eagles.

- He left Nigerian side Kwara for Norwegian side Brann in 2003.

- He was set to sign for French side Monaco for £2.5m but when talks broke down the Tigers stepped in with a successful £3m bid.

- Seyi is a graduate of Chemical Engineering from the Ladoke Akintola University.

- Seyi has taken part in two African Cup of Nations, though missed the 2006 tournament due to injury.

- Away from football the 6ft 4in midfielder regularly helps those less fortunate than himself and donates anonymously to various charitable causes.

10 THINGS YOU MIGHT (OR MIGHT NOT) KNOW ABOUT NICK BARMBY

- Nicky was born in Hull on 11 February 1974 and was a regular attender of City's home games as a kid.

- He attended Kelvin Hall High School in the city.

- He signed schoolboy forms for Tottenham Hotspur and made his debut v the Tigers during Garreth Roberts' testimonial at Boothferry Park – scoring two goals!

- It would be 13 years before he eventually joined his hometown club, signing for the Tigers in 2004.

- In 1995 he became Middlesbrough's record signing when he joined Boro for £5.25m and he scored the first ever goal at the Riverside Stadium.

- He became Everton's record signing 17 months later joining for £5.75m.

- Nicky then did the unthinkable by leaving Goodison Park for Liverpool for a £6m fee in 2000 – the first time in 41 years that the Toffees had sold a player to their deadly rivals!

- In 2002 he signed for Leeds United – managed by his first-ever boss Terry Venables.

- He scored the fastest goal in Tigers' history by netting after just 7 seconds against Walsall in 2004.

- Of his 23 England caps, one came during the historic 5–1 win away to Germany.

10 THINGS YOU MIGHT (OR MIGHT NOT) KNOW ABOUT ROBERT KOREN

- He began his career with Dravograd in Slovenia before moving to Norwegian side Lillestrom.

- His boyhood hero is Slovenian footballer Zlatko Zahovic.

- By the start of the 2012/13 season, Koren had won 61 caps for his country and scored 5 goals – he announced his retirement from international football in February 2012.

- In July 2007, Koren was temporarily blinded when a ball hit him in the eye – thankfully his sight returned shortly after.

- He has two sons and one daughter.

- Koren bagged the Player of the Year and Goal of the Season awards in his second season with the Tigers.

- City's coveted No. 10 signed a new two-year-deal in 2012.

- His home town of Radlje ob Dravi has a population of less than 5,000.

- Koren signed for West Brom on a Bosman deal and then joined City on a free transfer meaning he hasn't cost any of his English clubs a penny in transfer fees.

- His first Tigers goal was against Derby County in 2010

BRIAN MARWOOD –
10 THINGS YOU DIDN'T KNOW ABOUT
THE FORMER TIGERS WINGER

- Brian Marwood's autobiography was called *The Life of Brian*.

- Marwood made his debut against Mansfield Town on 12 January 1980.

- Scored Hull's two goals on the final day of the 1983/84 season. A third would have seen City promoted. This was his last game for the club.

- He left Boothferry Park for Sheffield Wednesday in a deal worth £115,000 after eight years with the Tigers at youth and senior level.

- He quit Hillsborough for Highbury when he joined Arsenal for £800,000 in 1988.

- His son, James, used to play for Newcastle United.

- Marwood gained his only international cap in a friendly against Saudi Arabia.

- He became a commentator for the BBC and Sky Sports before moving away from football to concentrate on business.

- He was Chairman of the PFA from 1990 to 1993.

- Since retirement he has worked for Nike but is currently back in football, employed by Manchester City as a football administrator.

TIGERS' COMPLETE LEAGUE RECORD

Below, beginning with the most recent campaign, is the complete statistical record of Hull City in League football:

P	W	D	L	F	A	W	D	L	F	A	W	D	L	F	A	Pts

2011/2012 Championship
8th

| 46 | 19 | 11 | 16 | 47 | 44 | 12 | 4 | 7 | 28 | 22 | 7 | 7 | 9 | 19 | 22 | 68 |

2010/2011 Championship
11th

| 46 | 16 | 17 | 13 | 52 | 51 | 7 | 8 | 8 | 21 | 19 | 9 | 9 | 5 | 31 | 32 | 65 |

2009/2010 Premier League
19th

| 38 | 6 | 12 | 20 | 34 | 75 | 6 | 6 | 7 | 22 | 29 | 0 | 6 | 13 | 12 | 46 | 30 |

2008/2009 Premier League
17th

| 38 | 3 | 5 | 11 | 18 | 36 | 5 | 6 | 8 | 21 | 28 | 8 | 11 | 19 | 39 | 64 | 35 |

2007/2008 Championship
3rd*

| 46 | 13 | 7 | 3 | 43 | 19 | 8 | 5 | 10 | 22 | 28 | 21 | 12 | 13 | 65 | 47 | 75 |

P	W	D	L	F	A	W	D	L	F	A	W	D	L	F	A	Pts

2006/2007 Championship
21st

P	W	D	L	F	A	W	D	L	F	A	W	D	L	F	A	Pts
46	8	3	12	33	32	5	7	11	18	35	13	10	23	51	67	49

2005/2006 Championship
18th

46	8	8	7	24	21	4	8	11	25	34	12	16	18	49	55	52

2004/2005 League One
2nd

46	16	5	2	42	17	10	3	10	38	36	26	8	12	80	53	86

2003/2004 Division Three
2nd

46	16	4	3	50	21	9	9	5	32	23	25	13	8	82	44	88

2002/2003 Division Three
13th

46	9	10	4	34	19	5	7	11	24	34	14	17	15	58	53	59

2001/2002 Division Three
11th

46	12	6	5	38	18	4	7	12	19	33	16	13	17	57	51	61

2000/2001 Division Three
6th

46	12	7	4	27	18	7	10	6	20	21	19	17	10	47	39	74

1999/2000 Division Three
14th

46	7	8	8	26	23	8	6	9	17	20	15	14	17	43	43	59

P	W	D	L	F	A	W	D	L	F	A	W	D	L	F	A	Pts

1998/1999 Division Three
21st

P	W	D	L	F	A	W	D	L	F	A	W	D	L	F	A	Pts
46	8	5	10	25	28	6	6	11	19	34	14	11	21	44	62	53

1997/1998 Division Three
22nd

46	10	6	7	36	32	1	2	20	20	51	11	8	27	56	83	41

1996/1997 Division Three
17th

46	9	8	6	29	26	4	10	9	15	24	13	18	15	44	50	57

1995/1996 Division Two
24th

46	4	8	11	26	37	1	8	14	10	41	5	16	25	36	78	31

1994/1995 Division Two
8th

46	13	6	4	40	18	8	5	10	30	39	21	11	14	70	57	74

1993/1994 Division Two
9th

46	9	9	5	33	20	9	5	9	29	34	18	14	14	62	54	68

1992/1993 Division Two
20th

46	9	5	9	28	26	4	6	13	18	43	13	11	22	46	69	50

1991/1992 Third Division
14th

46	9	4	10	28	23	7	7	9	26	31	16	11	19	54	54	59

P	W	D	L	F	A	W	D	L	F	A	W	D	L	F	A	Pts

1990/1991 Second Division
24th

| 46 | 6 | 10 | 7 | 35 | 32 | 4 | 5 | 14 | 22 | 53 | 10 | 15 | 21 | 57 | 85 | 45 |

1989/1990 Second Division
14th

| 46 | 7 | 8 | 8 | 27 | 31 | 7 | 8 | 8 | 31 | 34 | 14 | 16 | 16 | 58 | 65 | 58 |

1988/1989 Second Division
21st

| 46 | 7 | 9 | 7 | 31 | 25 | 4 | 5 | 14 | 21 | 43 | 11 | 14 | 21 | 52 | 68 | 47 |

1987/1988 Second Division
15th

| 44 | 10 | 8 | 4 | 32 | 22 | 4 | 7 | 11 | 22 | 38 | 14 | 15 | 15 | 54 | 60 | 57 |

1986/1987 Second Division
14th

| 42 | 10 | 6 | 5 | 25 | 22 | 3 | 8 | 10 | 16 | 33 | 13 | 14 | 15 | 41 | 55 | 53 |

1985/1986 Second Division
6th

| 42 | 11 | 7 | 3 | 39 | 19 | 6 | 6 | 9 | 26 | 36 | 17 | 13 | 12 | 65 | 55 | 64 |

1984/1985 Third Division
3rd

| 46 | 16 | 4 | 3 | 46 | 20 | 9 | 8 | 6 | 32 | 29 | 25 | 12 | 9 | 78 | 49 | 87 |

1983/1984 Third Division
4th

| 46 | 16 | 5 | 2 | 42 | 11 | 7 | 9 | 7 | 29 | 27 | 23 | 14 | 9 | 71 | 38 | 83 |

P	W	D	L	F	A	W	D	L	F	A	W	D	L	F	A	Pts

1982/1983 Fourth Division
2nd

P	W	D	L	F	A	W	D	L	F	A	W	D	L	F	A	Pts
46	14	8	1	48	14	11	7	5	27	20	25	15	6	75	34	90

1981/1982 Fourth Division
8th

46	14	3	6	36	23	5	9	9	34	38	19	12	15	70	61	69

1980/1981 Third Division
24th

46	7	8	8	23	22	1	8	14	17	49	8	16	22	40	71	32

1979/1980 Third Division
20th

46	11	7	5	29	21	1	9	13	22	48	12	16	18	51	69	40

1978/1979 Third Division
8th

46	12	9	2	36	14	7	2	14	30	47	19	11	16	66	61	49

1977/1978 Second Division
22nd

42	6	6	9	23	25	2	6	13	11	27	8	12	22	34	52	28

1976/1977 Second Division
14th

42	9	8	4	31	17	1	9	11	14	36	10	17	15	45	53	37

1975/1976 Second Division
14th

42	9	5	7	29	23	5	6	10	16	26	14	11	17	45	49	39

P	W	D	L	F	A	W	D	L	F	A	W	D	L	F	A	Pts

1974/1975 Second Division
8th

P	W	D	L	F	A	W	D	L	F	A	W	D	L	F	A	Pts
42	12	8	1	25	10	3	6	12	15	43	15	14	13	40	53	44

1973/1974 Second Division
9th

| 42 | 9 | 9 | 3 | 25 | 15 | 4 | 8 | 9 | 21 | 32 | 13 | 17 | 12 | 46 | 47 | 43 |

1972/1973 Second Division
13th

| 42 | 9 | 7 | 5 | 39 | 22 | 5 | 5 | 11 | 25 | 37 | 14 | 12 | 16 | 64 | 59 | 40 |

1971/1972 Second Division
12th

| 42 | 10 | 6 | 5 | 33 | 21 | 4 | 4 | 13 | 16 | 32 | 14 | 10 | 18 | 49 | 53 | 38 |

1970/1971 Second Division
5th

| 42 | 11 | 5 | 5 | 31 | 16 | 8 | 8 | 5 | 23 | 25 | 19 | 13 | 10 | 54 | 41 | 51 |

1969/1970 Second Division
13th

| 42 | 11 | 6 | 4 | 43 | 28 | 4 | 5 | 12 | 29 | 42 | 15 | 11 | 16 | 72 | 70 | 41 |

1968/1969 Second Division
11th

| 42 | 10 | 7 | 4 | 38 | 20 | 3 | 9 | 9 | 21 | 32 | 13 | 16 | 13 | 59 | 52 | 42 |

1967/1968 Second Division
17th

| 42 | 6 | 8 | 7 | 25 | 23 | 6 | 5 | 10 | 33 | 50 | 12 | 13 | 17 | 58 | 73 | 37 |

P	W	D	L	F	A	W	D	L	F	A	W	D	L	F	A	Pts

1966/1967 Second Division
12th

| 42 | 11 | 5 | 5 | 46 | 25 | 5 | 2 | 14 | 31 | 47 | 16 | 7 | 19 | 77 | 72 | 39 |

1965/1966 Third Division
1st

| 46 | 19 | 2 | 2 | 64 | 24 | 12 | 5 | 6 | 45 | 38 | 31 | 7 | 8 | 109 | 62 | 69 |

1964/1965 Third Division
4th

| 46 | 14 | 6 | 3 | 51 | 25 | 9 | 6 | 8 | 40 | 32 | 23 | 12 | 11 | 91 | 57 | 58 |

1963/1964 Third Division
8th

| 46 | 11 | 9 | 3 | 45 | 27 | 5 | 8 | 10 | 28 | 41 | 16 | 17 | 13 | 73 | 68 | 49 |

1962/1963 Third Division
10th

| 46 | 12 | 6 | 5 | 40 | 22 | 7 | 4 | 12 | 34 | 47 | 19 | 10 | 17 | 74 | 69 | 48 |

1961/1962 Third Division
10th

| 46 | 15 | 2 | 6 | 43 | 20 | 5 | 6 | 12 | 24 | 34 | 20 | 8 | 18 | 67 | 54 | 48 |

1960/1961 Third Division
11th

| 46 | 13 | 6 | 4 | 51 | 28 | 4 | 6 | 13 | 22 | 45 | 17 | 12 | 17 | 73 | 73 | 46 |

1959/1960 Second Division
21st

| 42 | 7 | 6 | 8 | 27 | 30 | 3 | 4 | 14 | 21 | 46 | 10 | 10 | 22 | 48 | 76 | 30 |

P	W	D	L	F	A	W	D	L	F	A	W	D	L	F	A	Pts

1958/1959 Third Division
2nd

P	W	D	L	F	A	W	D	L	F	A	W	D	L	F	A	Pts
46	19	3	1	65	21	7	6	10	25	34	26	9	11	90	55	61

1957/1958 Third Division (N)
5th

46	15	6	2	49	20	4	9	10	29	47	19	15	12	78	67	53

1956/1957 Third Division (N)
8th

46	14	6	3	45	24	7	4	12	39	45	21	10	15	84	69	52

1955/1956 Second Division
22nd

42	6	4	11	32	45	4	2	15	21	52	10	6	26	53	97	26

1954/1955 Second Division
19th/22

42	7	5	9	30	35	5	5	11	14	34	12	10	20	44	69	34

1953/1954 Second Division
15th/22

42	14	1	6	47	22	2	5	14	17	44	16	6	20	64	66	38

1952/1953 Second Division
18th/22

42	11	6	4	36	19	3	2	16	21	50	14	8	20	57	69	36

1951/1952 Second Division
18th/22

42	11	5	5	44	23	2	6	13	16	47	13	11	18	60	70	37

P	W	D	L	F	A	W	D	L	F	A	W	D	L	F	A	Pts

1950/1951 Second Division
10th/22

| 42 | 12 | 5 | 4 | 47 | 28 | 4 | 6 | 11 | 27 | 42 | 16 | 11 | 15 | 74 | 70 | 43 |

1949/1950 Second Division
7th/22

| 42 | 11 | 8 | 2 | 39 | 25 | 6 | 3 | 12 | 25 | 47 | 17 | 11 | 14 | 64 | 72 | 45 |

1948/1949 Third Division (N)
1st/22

| 42 | 17 | 1 | 3 | 65 | 14 | 10 | 10 | 1 | 28 | 14 | 27 | 11 | 4 | 93 | 28 | 65 |

1947/1948 Third Division (N)
5th/22

| 42 | 12 | 5 | 4 | 38 | 21 | 6 | 6 | 9 | 21 | 27 | 18 | 11 | 13 | 59 | 48 | 47 |

1946/1947 Third Division (N)
11th/22

| 42 | 9 | 5 | 7 | 25 | 19 | 7 | 3 | 11 | 24 | 34 | 16 | 8 | 18 | 49 | 53 | 40 |

1938/1939 Third Division (N)
7th/22

| 42 | 13 | 5 | 3 | 57 | 25 | 5 | 5 | 11 | 26 | 49 | 18 | 10 | 14 | 83 | 74 | 46 |

1937/1938 Third Division (N)
3rd/22

| 42 | 11 | 8 | 2 | 51 | 19 | 9 | 5 | 7 | 29 | 24 | 20 | 13 | 9 | 80 | 43 | 53 |

1936/1937 Third Division (N)
5th/22

| 42 | 13 | 6 | 2 | 39 | 22 | 4 | 6 | 11 | 29 | 47 | 17 | 12 | 13 | 68 | 69 | 46 |

P	W	D	L	F	A	W	D	L	F	A	W	D	L	F	A	Pts

1935/1936 Second Division
22nd

P	W	D	L	F	A	W	D	L	F	A	W	D	L	F	A	Pts
42	4	7	10	33	45	1	3	17	14	66	5	10	27	47	111	20

1934/1935 Second Division
13th

42	9	6	6	32	22	7	2	12	31	52	16	8	18	63	74	40

1933/1934 Second Division
15th

42	11	4	6	33	20	2	8	11	19	48	13	12	17	52	68	38

1932/1933 Third Division (N)
1st

42	18	3	0	69	14	8	4	9	31	31	26	7	9	100	45	59

1931/1932 Third Division (N)
8th/21

40	14	1	5	52	21	6	4	10	30	32	20	5	15	82	53	45

1930/1931 Third Division (N)
6th

42	12	7	2	64	20	8	3	10	35	35	20	10	12	99	55	50

1929/1930 Second Division
21st

42	11	3	7	30	24	3	4	14	21	54	14	7	21	51	78	35

1928/1929 Second Division
12th

42	8	8	5	38	24	5	6	10	20	39	13	14	15	58	63	40

P	W	D	L	F	A	W	D	L	F	A	W	D	L	F	A	Pts

1927/1928 Second Division
14th

P	W	D	L	F	A	W	D	L	F	A	W	D	L	F	A	Pts
42	9	8	4	25	19	3	7	11	16	35	12	15	15	41	54	39

1926/1927 Second Division
7th

42	13	4	4	43	19	7	3	11	20	33	20	7	15	63	52	47

1925/1926 Second Division
13th

42	11	4	6	40	19	5	5	11	23	42	16	9	17	63	61	41

1924/1925 Second Division
10th

42	12	6	3	40	14	3	5	13	10	35	15	11	16	50	49	41

1923/1924 Second Division
17th

42	8	7	6	32	23	2	10	9	14	28	10	17	15	46	51	37

1922/1923 Second Division
12th

42	9	8	4	29	22	5	6	10	14	23	14	14	14	43	45	42

1921/1922 Second Division
5th

42	13	5	3	36	13	6	5	10	15	28	19	10	13	51	41	48

1920/1921 Second Division
13th

42	7	10	4	24	18	3	10	8	19	35	10	20	12	43	53	40

P	W	D	L	F	A	W	D	L	F	A	W	D	L	F	A	Pts

1919/1920 Second Division
11th

P	W	D	L	F	A	W	D	L	F	A	W	D	L	F	A	Pts
42	13	4	4	53	23	5	2	14	25	49	18	6	18	78	72	42

1914/1915 Second Division
7th

38	12	2	5	36	23	7	3	9	29	31	19	5	14	65	54	43

1913/1914 Second Division
7th

38	9	5	5	29	13	7	4	8	24	24	16	9	13	53	37	41

1912/1913 Second Division
12th

38	12	2	5	42	18	3	4	12	18	37	15	6	17	60	55	36

1911/1912 Second Division
7th

38	12	3	4	36	13	5	5	9	18	38	17	8	13	54	51	42

1910/1911 Second Division
5th

38	8	10	1	38	21	6	6	7	17	18	14	16	8	55	39	44

1909/1910 Second Division
3rd

38	13	4	2	52	19	10	3	6	28	27	23	7	8	80	46	53

1908/1909 Second Division
4th

38	14	2	3	44	15	5	4	10	19	24	19	6	13	63	39	44